THE
POWER
OF
FOOD

THE
POWER
OF
FOOD

100 Essential Recipes for Abundant Health and Happiness

ADAM HART

FOREWORD BY DAVID WOLFE

whitecap

Whitecap Books is known for its expertise in the cookbook market, and has produced some
of the most innovative and familiar titles found in kitchens across North America.
Visit our website at www.whitecap.ca.

EDITED BY: Theresa Best and Naomi Pauls
DESIGN BY: Andrew Bagatella
COVER DESIGN BY: Naomi MacDougall
COVER PHOTOGRAPH BY: Brad Wenner
PHOTOGRAPHY BY: Nick Sopczak (www.nicksopczakphotography.com)
RECIPE PHOTOGRAPHY BY: Michelle Furbacher

Printed in Canada

Library and Archives Canada Cataloguing in Publication

Hart, Adam, 1973-
    The power of food : 100 essential recipes for abundant health and happiness
/ Adam Hart.

Includes index.
ISBN 978-1-77050-182-9

1. Cooking. 2. Health. 3. Mind and body. 4. Cookbooks. I. Title.

TX714.H369 2013   641.5'63   C2013-900086-0

The publisher acknowledges the financial support of the Government of Canada through
the Canada Book Fund (CBF) and the Province of British Columbia through the Book
Publishing Tax Credit.

13 14 15 16 17   5 4 3 2 1

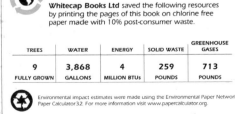

To my daughter,

Juliette, whose smile

melts my heart.

TABLE OF

CONTENTS

FOREWORD

BY DAVID WOLFE

STEP-BY-STEP, progress and innovation are happening and the rate at which they are happening is accelerating. The dramatic increase in our ability to communicate with each other has led to a transformation in knowledge— what has been experienced can be shared so rapidly now.

Two hundred years ago, the concept of changing one's diet, in the way that is possible today, did not exist, and there were only a few limited ways to communicate dietary experiences. Now, millions of people have spent significant amounts of time experimenting with different diets and nutrition strategies. They have shared their experiences with others in ways that were simply not possible before. We now know that food has the "power" to help us heal, that how we grow and treat our food is important to our health, that we can improve our health by taking intelligent actions daily and that the quality of food counts.

What I love about Adam Hart's *The Power of Food* is that it is much more than a book about diet. Adam asks questions about where our food comes from and how our food is grown. And he explains that raw and "living" foods are important in developing and nurturing the connected, life-force energies that help us manifest our dreams.

Transformation is possible for all of us. And it is getting easier. More and more tools are being provided, but it is important to be able to feel the grace of opportunity that surrounds us. Begin to get into the mindset that will allow you to feel that grace. Right now, as you read these words, you can begin to powerfully and positively transform your life and the lives of those around you. This is possible, as Adam says, when you commit to taking action.

In *The Power of Food,* you will discover that health and wellness are products of actions. And you will be encouraged to take action—by following the 12 action steps in this book, by keeping a *Daily Food Journal,* by eating from the six food categories highlighted, by selecting Power Foods and by fully experiencing the wide array of easy-to-follow recipes!

The Power of Food is Adam Hart's own story—his own experience—of discovering how important the correct foods are for activating our full human potential. Soak in the book's knowledge—as the roots of sprouts soak in water—and see what extraordinary things can grow in the garden of your life as a result. Enjoy *The Power of Food* and have the best day ever!

—David "Avocado" Wolfe (davidwolfe.com), author of
Superfoods: The Food and Medicine of the Future

PREFACE

I WAS ONCE VERY UNHEALTHY—pre-diabetic, overweight and suffering from mental illness in the form of depression and anxiety attacks. However, I was able to regain control over my own health after I discovered the power of food. This discovery allowed me to begin living my life from a place of pure happiness. It was food that helped me begin to understand my ability to heal myself.

I wrote *The Power of Food* to share with you everything I discovered along my 10-year journey to living with abundant health. Along the way, I adopted a style of eating that places no restrictions on your diet or lifestyle yet has proven results. I share this discovery and the system I used, to make it easier for you to experience the results you desire long-term.

The Power of Food takes you through several years of my life and describes the 12 action steps I implemented to begin living each day full of energy and loving my life. The story begins with my childhood and spans 40 years to the present. At the age of 28 I began to discover a way of life that helped me to reverse my pre-diabetic state, remove my daily need for high-cholesterol medication, quit a 13-year smoking habit, eliminate my severe food allergies and reduce the impact of depression and anxiety on my life. Throughout *The Power of Food* you will find tips, secrets, tools and resources that will help you too create a healthier lifestyle.

In hundreds of public and private events as a professional speaker, I have had many requests to share more of my story. I wrote *The Power of Food* for you, and I look forward to being a part of your success.

The Power of Food is in your hands thanks to my beautiful wife, Suzie, who supports me with all her heart. My mother, Honey, is a beacon of light who has gifted me with abundance and to whom I am forever grateful. I also thank my entire Toronto, Quebec, Golden and Squamish family. You are all a part of my energy and I love you all. I also thank my publisher, Whitecap Books, for sharing *The Power of Food* with you, and thank my entire publishing team for their support and encouragement.

Adam

INTRODUCTION

DID YOU WAKE UP THIS MORNING feeling a little tired? Would you like to wake up tomorrow morning ready to attack your day like a lion, full of strength and energy? These are the two questions I pose to audience members during my Power of Food live events. The most common answers I hear are yes and yes. Many audience members share personal stories about their health struggles and desire for more energy. I know how each of them feels, for I once suffered in much the same way. As you will learn through *The Power of Food,* food is your lifeline to waking up each morning with supercharged energy.

How is it that something as simple as eating can cause so many people frustration and stress? The problem lies in choosing the right types of food for healthier eating. We all have to eat to survive, but we don't always make the best food choices. Over the past 50 years many North Americans have taken the enjoyment of processed foods to new heights. So it's no surprise that when we take a good look at those around us, we see a lot of overworked, overstressed and overweight friends, family members, neighbours, co-workers and children.

We have become a society disconnected from our food as well as from our ability to live with a sense of purpose and joy. This has left many of us unconsciously struggling to feel alive and healthy. I am here to tell you that life doesn't have to be this way for you. You have the ability *right now* to start looking great and feeling even

better. I can say this with confidence because I have regained control over my own health through the power of food of.

It's no secret that I was not always a beacon of health and happiness. Not too long ago I suffered from several health issues that made me feel unworthy and unwanted. I was starving for answers to help me overcome my many ailments. I spent more than 10 years seeking the answers that have enabled me to live each day with abundant energy. This book is my gift to you, in which I share the tips, tools, secrets and powerful systems I learned and adopted to gain abundant health. You can use them to do the same. My personal story is a great starting point to help inspire, motivate, encourage and support you in your journey to living each day with supercharged energy. In the pages that follow I also share the 12 action steps that became part of my personal healing story and have allowed thousands of others to tap into a heightened level of energy.

My story represents living proof that we all have a purpose in life. Like many of you I spent years wondering what I was meant to be doing with my life. Discovering the power within food opened up a world I had never imagined possible. What I discovered helped me to lose over 40 pounds, reverse my pre-diabetic state, quit smoking, get off high-cholesterol medication, eliminate anaphylactic food allergies, stop my attention-deficit/

hyperactivity disorder and alleviate my depression and anxiety attacks. If you too implement each of the 12 action steps and make them a part of your life, you can expect to experience some very powerful results. A rise in your energy levels is usually the most common benefit. You will experience this not in a matter of years or months, but within days of reading *The Power of Food*.

And if you think my approach is difficult, think again. The idea that getting healthy is hard and takes a lot of work is outdated. The reality is, every thought you have is either an act of love or not. *The Power of Food* will teach you how to love, care for and respect your food so you can love, care for and respect yourself on a deeper, more energized level. This mindset gives you access to your body's own healing power of reading *The Power of Food*.

Do you want to be free of your food addictions or your food and sugar cravings? No matter what you suffer from, be it diabetes, cancer, heart disease, arthritis, poor quality of sleep, irritable bowel syndrome, constant fatigue, depression or anxiety, *The Power of Food* will improve your overall health and get your energy flowing. It's time to supercharge your life. Let's get started!

MY JOURNEY TO BETTER HEALTH

FROM A VERY YOUNG AGE I had a poor relationship with food. This relationship started with me getting food as a reward. Take a moment to think about all the foods you ate when you were young. Sugary cereals, ice cream, chocolate, cookies, chips and pop are the most common foods I hear about from audience members and coaching clients. The big reward for me as a child was fast food. If my sister and I behaved we got to go to McDonald's to eat. It is common to this day for parents to feed their children processed and refined foods that cost little, taste good and are quick and convenient.

In the past it was hard to fault parents for this practice, because very little knowledge was readily available about the power of food. This has changed in the past 20 years. Thanks to the World Wide Web, we now have access to unlimited resources to discover all we need to know to look after our loved ones and ourselves. So why do so many parents continue to feed their children fast food and processed foods? This is a deep question whose answer could fill an entire book, but two of the main reasons are lack of time and lack of energy. Yes, the knowledge about healthy foods is available, but we often lack the time to do our own research, and when we do have the time, we are sometimes too tired to put our research to good use.

I am a great example of what can happen when you feed your child a daily dose of processed and refined foods. My poor eating habits as a child led to my addiction to processed, harmful foods devoid of nutrients. Around the age of 12 I was diagnosed with attention-deficit/hyperactivity disorder (ADHD). In school it was commonplace for teachers to pull me out of class and put me into a separate room where I could "think" about my behaviour. This was both traumatic and humiliating for me. Throughout my teenage years I battled with keeping up in school, always feeling like I had to work harder than all of the other kids just to make the grade. At the age of 13 I was put on Ritalin, a pharmaceutical that aims to increase focus on tasks, reduce hyperactive behaviour and curb impulsivity. I was drugged to help control my ADHD. All the while I had been consuming heavily processed foods that provided very little in nutritional value and left me starving for strength, energy and brainpower.

So I ask you, was I suffering from ADHD or from a lack of essential nutrients due to poor food choices? I now know that a lack of nutrient consumption as a child resulted in my ADHD diagnosis and helps to explain why so many children today are being treated for ADHD.

My poor relationship with food continued as I put myself through university in Toronto. During my university days I spent much of my time either shooting pool or studying in the library. I also spent lots of my time surrounded by the smell of pizza, for to help pay my way through university, I took a job at a pizza restaurant.

When I was growing up, pizza was a staple in our family's kitchen. It just so happens that I became the manager of this pizza restaurant.

Of course, as manager of the restaurant, I had access to as much pizza as I could possibly eat. And as a young university student with very little cash, I took full advantage of my position. I took such good advantage that by the age of 22 I had reached a weight of 198 pounds, a full 40 pounds heavier than I am today. On a 5'11" frame that's not too bad, but I was overweight and lacking energy.

Eventually I graduated from York University with a degree in sociology, and I earned a postgraduate diploma in international business management from Seneca College, also in Toronto. I left my pizza job upon graduation and entered the real working world. At 24 years old and still not really knowing myself or what I was capable of becoming, I found this move into the "rat race" came as a pretty big shock to my system, and my health took the full impact in a very negative way.

SLAVE TO THE TRAFFIC LIGHTS

With all the time I spent shooting pool and eating pizza during my post-secondary years, perhaps it is not so surprising that I was able to graduate with no real clue as to my purpose in life. Where was I headed? What was I now going to do with my nicely framed degree and diploma? Confused about my life's purpose, I decided to take the easy route and enter the family business. This was a no-brainer for a recent graduate who really had no idea what to do next. My uncles, who owned an upscale furniture store in Toronto, offered me a position as operations manager.

I settled into my white-walled office looking forward to the challenge ahead. But I was in for a real surprise. My office was a room with no windows, carpet that looked as if it had been salvaged from a demolition site, air circulation comparable to that in an airplane, and a constant computer buzz able to drill a hole directly into my temples. And that's where I had the pleasure of working 8 to 10 hours a day, six days a week, getting a second day off every other week. Working for family you would think things would be a little easier, but as I found out very quickly, the situation was just the opposite. Within six months of being in charge of up to 30 employees, I was suffering from extreme stress.

ACTION STEP 1.
CALM THE STORM

In early 2000 I began to realize the power of my breath and developed a breathing strategy to help me stay calm in stressful situations. This practice did not always work at first, but the more I engaged it, the more powerful it became. Here's how to do it.

1. Think about the top three stressors or locations where you feel the most stress in your life.
2. Write down the word BREATHE three times on three pieces of paper, while breathing in and out slowly.
3. Place the papers in the three locations. Maybe you experience stress at your workstation, inside your car (traffic was my big stressor) or in your kitchen.
4. Every time you feel your shoulders getting tense, your breath getting short and your frustration or anger rising, look at your BREATHE note, take in three deep breaths and continue on with your day.

WHAT YOU CAN EXPECT: Your shoulders will relax, and you will feel lighter, calmer and more energized. This very powerful act of love for yourself will allow you to approach your main stressors from a new angle and reduce their negative impact on your overall well-being.

Stress has become an epidemic in our society. Along with our disconnection from food, stress leads to the majority of ailments and diseases we suffer from today. Not too long after my stress levels increased, I started experiencing bouts of depression as well as anxiety attacks. In addition, I had been fighting with asthma for many years, and now, all of a sudden, I was diagnosed with fresh fruit syndrome.

What is that? This was the question screaming in my mind while I tried to come to grips with my declining health. To my surprise my unhealthy state was causing my immune system to crash, and my body had started rejecting many of the foods I had enjoyed eating for years. I suddenly became allergic to apples, peaches, pears, plums, carrots, celery and all different kinds of nuts. After doing much research on allergies I came to realize that the more you test food allergies, the worse they can become. Boy, did I find that out the hard way, having my one and only anaphylactic reaction after eating a hazelnut back in the year 2000.

Allergies are an autoimmune dysfunction. The stronger your immune system becomes, the weaker your allergies will be. I know that fact now because many of my food allergies have been downgraded from anaphylactic to minor intolerances or eliminated altogether. I credit the strengthening of my immune system over the past 10 years with reversing my once debilitating food allergies.

Well, there I was, 26 years old, living in an overweight body, extremely stressed, experiencing bouts of depression and anxiety attacks, struggling for a decent breath of air thanks to my asthma and unable to eat many of the foods I loved due to my fresh fruit syndrome. If all that was not enough, I walked into my doctor's office one fateful day in late 2000 and got another big slap in the face. My doctor handed me a prescription for high-cholesterol medication.

Now I have high cholesterol to add to my list? I thought. I stood in front of my doctor with a shocked look on my face and proceeded to ask, "What does high cholesterol mean?"

"Adam, take this prescription and get it filled. Start on the medication immediately and you will have nothing to worry about." In frustration I blurted out, "But I am already taking several medications. Why another one?" I was shocked to hear my doctor say: "Adam, you are pre-diabetic. If you do not begin taking this medication right away, you could potentially be insulin dependent within six months."

Great, so there I was—pre-diabetic as well. I had no idea what high cholesterol meant or what being diabetic was all about. I was stuck with the realization that I would have to rely on even more medication. I walked out of my doctor's office totally dejected and frustrated, feeling like a complete failure. My body had been slowly decaying and now my mind had joined in. Welcome to rock bottom, Adam, and you're only 26 years old. I spiralled deeper into depression for several months while trying to get a grip on my unhealthy state.

RECONNECTING TO MY OWN HEALTH

Several weeks after leaving my doctor's office, I was sitting in a coffee shop, daydreaming, when I clued into something I had never noticed before. *I was not alone.* I took a good look around the coffee shop and saw a gentleman in the far right corner with four different pills sitting on the table ready to be popped. To my left sat a hunched-over elderly woman breathing with the assistance of an oxygen tank, and right beside me was a young girl wearing a medical bracelet for an allergy to nuts. It dawned on me at that moment: not only was I not alone, but many of my friends, family members, co-workers, neighbours and fellow coffee shop patrons were all on similar unhealthy paths. My story was not unique, and I felt a little inspired to move away from feeling sorry for myself and to begin taking action.

How is it that so many of us have become disconnected from our own health? Not knowing it at the time, I have since discovered that my path to better health came through reconnecting to the foods I ate. Caring more about the foods I ate while at the same time engaging my intentions around what I wanted my life to become, I began to shift my dominant negative thoughts into positive, uplifting and motivating ones. Eating unhealthy food contributed to my daily negative thoughts, which conditioned me to live the life of a *human doing*, far from the powerful and energizing existence of a *human being*.

AFFIRM YOUR GREATNESS

I began using this exercise in 2001, once I finally allowed some positive light to enter my formerly dark world. It did not always make me feel better at first, but the more I practised it, the more it allowed me to honour myself and the more it gave me confidence. Try it for yourself.

1. Take a nice long deep breath in *right now.*
2. Close your eyes and take another long deep breath in and let it out very slowly.
3. With your eyes closed, visualize in your mind the one thing you are most proud of achieving in your life. Is it the birth of your child? Maybe you passed an exam or got your driver's licence. Perhaps you met a health goal or started going after one. Whatever you are proudest of right now, see it in your mind.
4. With your eyes still closed, take another deep breath in and begin curving the outer parts of your mouth upwards as you breathe out. Yes, you are now smiling.
5. Keep your eyes closed for the next 20 to 30 seconds while you enjoy breathing in your greatness as you smile for your heart to see. Visualize your achievement and relive it in your mind.
6. Repeat steps 1 to 5 two more times today.

WHAT YOU CAN EXPECT: This exercise might feel a bit strange at first, but it brings positive results. The more you bring what I call "Mindful Moments" into your daily program, the more energy you will have, the happier you will feel and the healthier you will become. How will you know if it is working? Well, how do you feel after doing it? There's your proof.

HUMAN DOING VS. HUMAN BEING

For many years I lived with blinders over my eyes, each day struggling just to survive. Does living as a *human doing* rather than a *human being* relate to you as well? My daily priorities consisted of paying my bills, getting my hands on the next hot technological advancement, driving a nice car and watching television on my flat-screen plasma TV. During this time I was never really concerned for my health. Yet at 26 years of age, my body and mind had hit a major roadblock. My unhealthy situation was a direct result of living as a *human doing* rather than as a *human being.*

Using medication to numb the pain of my unconscious, unhealthy life was a conspiracy I had played a role in for quite some time. However, hitting rock bottom allowed me to take the blinders off my eyes and witness the life I was living. My moment of clarity came while sitting in the coffee shop, noticing I was not alone in my unhealthy suffering. I found myself inspired to take a good hard look at my life and consciously decided to take action. I was tired of giving up control over my health to countless diets, cleanses, supplements and medications while listening to the media, doctors, family and friends tell me what to do next.

I did not want to be overweight anymore, I did not want to spend another night crying myself to sleep, I did not want to use prescription drugs to treat my ailments, and so on . . . Instead I wanted to start living my life with abundant energy. I wanted to wake up in the morning and not dread looking at myself in the mirror. I was tired of living a life feeling like a slave to the traffic lights. I was ready to let it all go and find my purpose in life. But to do so, I needed to say goodbye to the Adam I had known for 26 years and open my heart and mind to the limitless potential I knew existed within me.

ACTION STEP 3.
SET YOUR INTENTIONS

Through many of the business books I had read in university, I knew how setting intentions plays a key role in success. I had never done this before, but in 2000 I finally sat down and created a list of my 5-year intentions for myself. This initial list of intentions finally gave my life some direction. Setting intentions is the most powerful action step I can share with you. Since I first wrote down my intentions over 10 years ago, I have been continually moving forward, with some extremely exciting results.

1. Find a notebook you can use as your Power of Food Notebook.
2. On the cover draw a big heart in the middle and write overtop "I Love You." Okay, you men out there, I know what you may be thinking: Write "I Love You" on it—is this guy nuts? Don't be shy and don't let your ego get in the way. You can hide this journal so nobody sees it. It can be for your eyes only. Trust me and just do it.
3. On the first page of the journal, on the top line, write in capital letters "MY 5-YEAR INTENTIONS ARE..."
4. On the next few lines below your title, begin to list in point form where you would like to be five years from now. Leave about five empty lines below each intention you write. This list does not need to be long. You can write 5 points or 25 points. It's up to you. Think in terms of your health, relationships, career, finances, and so on.
5. Pick one intention on your list, and then close your eyes and visualize it in your mind for 20 seconds. Imagine exactly how you want that particular intention to look and feel for you as if it were happening right now.

6. Write down in the lines below each intention any extra clarity that came during your visualization.

7. Repeat steps 5 and 6 before you get out of bed each day this week.

WHAT YOU CAN EXPECT: I have been engaging my intentions this way for 10 years and I want you to know, it works! If you practise this exercise daily, it will inspire you, motivate you, excite you and energize you. It will guide you to your life's purpose. What do you have to lose? Give it a try right now.

The mind is the most powerful part of you. It is not what your eyes see, but what your mind creates for your eyes to see that is true brilliance manifested. Many years ago I would have thought this was a ridiculous concept, but today I know it is the truth. The sooner you believe, the sooner you will experience lasting healthy results.

To experience the true power of visualizing, you need to use your imagination. Our imagination is more powerful than many of us realize. Each of us creates our own reality, consciously or unconsciously. Either you choose to imagine and thereby move in the direction of your dreams, or you accept life as it comes, seemingly unaware of your profound ability to control and shape your life.

When you visualize an intention, it is important that you see it, imagine it and feel it as if you were truly experiencing it at that moment. If you practise visualization with complete awareness and belief, you will begin to manifest in your life all your intentions.

Visualizing does not require a lot of time. Even a one-minute visualization session will produce results. The more you practise visualizing, the easier you will find it to reach a state of deep relaxation where you then create your intention in a vision with the help of your imagination, exactly as you desire it to be. As you practise, be aware of the energy pouring over and through you. This is your connection to the Universe, and sharing in this energy will manifest your vision at a higher level. Sometimes I can't believe I am talking this way, coming from a place of being overweight, pre-diabetic and suffering with depression for many years, yet my transformative experience is the very reason why I can honestly share this information with you. I know it works.

You can use the power of visualization to imagine your way to whatever you want. Nothing within the realm of human accomplishment is impossible to you. The one important addition to your ability to manifest your vision is to believe. The more you believe without a doubt and act as though whatever you want is on its way, the sooner you will experience your every desire.

MY 5-YEAR INTENTIONS

Most of my thoughts in the past did not serve me in a positive way. Do any of these thoughts sound familiar? *Why does this always happen to me? When is it going to be my turn to. . .? It's not fair they always get. . . Why am I such a failure? Why can't anything go right?*

Angry at being overweight, upset from being depressed, sad at not being able to eat foods I had loved in the past and frustrated at being dependent on medication, I was caught in a vicious cycle of negative thoughts that fed off one another. Once I began to shift my daily thinking to the positive, I was able to create a little mental clarity. This clarity provided me with just enough light in my very dark world to ask myself, *What would I really like to be doing with my life?* Just as you have now done with Action Step 3, I sat down one day and wrote out my 5-year intentions. Here are a few of them—for the record.

- To live in a beautiful home
- To have a loving wife and children
- To be physically strong, active and fit
- To wake up energized and excited about life
- To have a successful business related to being outdoors

I practised visualizing my intentions for several months, as I wrote about in Action Step 3. This practice began to provide me with some much-needed clarity on what my next move should be. Instead of forcing myself into making decisions that might or might not have worked out, I allowed the Universe to bring the answers to me through my daily visualizations on what I wanted in my life. I began noticing that the more I gave myself the act of love by visualizing my intentions, the more images started to appear in my mind, helping me to fill in the details. That is why I tell all my clients today: you only need one starting intention to begin this empowering process. This book in your hands is testament to the power of intentions.

After a few months of embracing my intentions and becoming more clear about each one on my list, I saw that my next move was to honour myself by making a plan. I sat down and wrote out a detailed five-year action plan to recapture my health and go after my intentions. I am not suggesting you do this right now, but in due time, through daily practice with all the action steps found in *The Power of Food,* you will come to a point where creating an action plan will happen with ease.

My first year was to be spent saving up enough money to leave work and continue on my journey of self-discovery. Granted, at 26 years old I did not have a mortgage, children, a girlfriend or any other responsibilities that might have held me back from going after my intentions. But the truth is, such perceived obstacles are only excuses. I acknowledge everyone who feels trapped in their current situation, for I used to feel this way myself. Too many bills to pay, mouths to feed with very little time and a lack of energy to take care of yourself are excuses you can choose to make for yourself or not. Eventually your poor health will make the decision for you, as it did for me. To truly begin living a life of magic, you require unconditional trust, an ability to face your fears without any doubts of success and a strong belief that anything and everything is possible. Keep reading and I will tell you how I discovered a life of magic.

~~~~~~~~~

There are no limits. There are only plateaus, and you must not stay there, you must go beyond them. —Bruce Lee

LIFE IN THE MOUNTAINS

I was out with a friend one day in 1998 rollerblading in downtown Toronto. We were both overweight and looking for some activity that did not require us going to a gym. I had bought several gym memberships in the past, and they had always left me feeling guilty or frustrated. This was because after a few months of using the gym, I would start missing days in my gym routine. Every time I missed a day, I would feel depressed, and eventually I would stop going altogether. Spending time at a gym or doing any other fitness activity needs to be fun. If it is not, it is not the right way to spend your time. My friend and I were rollerblading as an alternative fitness routine when we happened to pass an indoor rock climbing gym.

Right away we looked at one another, big grins on both our faces, and decided to give the sport a try.

Being afraid of heights, I got halfway up the first climb we tried and asked to be let down. But something else happened to me on that very first day I tried indoor rock climbing. I was able to find just enough space between my thoughts to feel calm and relaxed. I was not sure what I had discovered, but I soon became very addicted to rock climbing. It was the first time in my life I was able to turn off my thoughts and just be in the moment. Plus, rock climbing was a lot of fun.

I grew attached to the feeling of peace and quiet in my mind every time I climbed. This feeling brought me back to the climbing gym time and time again, until I found myself heading outside to give the sport a try on real rock in early 2000. Climbing outdoors only strengthened my love for rock climbing, and I began a new relationship with nature that has nourished me on the deepest levels imaginable. I never knew the power of being with nature before I started outdoor rock climbing. As I spent more time with nature I began to breathe deeper and expand my consciousness, which eventually led me to an abundant life in the mountains.

ACTION STEP 4.
BE WITH NATURE

Since discovering the power of being with nature, I have used it daily to keep me calm, relaxed and connected to my inner ability to stay strong and healthy. Notice how I say "Be with Nature," not "Be in Nature." Being with nature holds more power, and this action step reveals how to do it.

1. Take a walk outside for five minutes.
2. Find a nice quiet spot where you can relax for two minutes sitting or standing in peace.
3. Once you stop, take three nice long deep breaths in and out very slowly.
4. Take a look around you and see what Mother Nature has put in front of your eyes. Do you see a tree, a flower, some rocks?
5. Pick something in nature you see before you and move a little closer to it.
6. Engaging all your senses, notice everything you can about your chosen piece of nature. Be as present with it as possible. Tune out all outside distractions and just "be" with your chosen item.
7. Take three nice long deep breaths in and release each one slowly while looking at your piece of nature.
8. Feel your piece of nature breathing with you and share your energy freely as you strengthen your connection to the power of life all around you.
9. Repeat steps 1 to 8 three times this week.

WHAT YOU CAN EXPECT: You will feel calmer, more relaxed and more deeply connected to the living energy all around you. You will sleep more soundly, wake feeling well rested and enjoy more energy. Your love of life will grow stronger and stronger every time you practise this action step.

Having begun to awaken the health within, thanks to engaging my intentions and spending a lot of time rock climbing, I decided to explore my options in the outdoor adventure world. I had spent almost one year saving money to leave the "rat race." The next step in my five-year plan was to give myself one year to break into the outdoor adventure industry. Since I had enjoyed rock climbing so

much, I decided to try another outdoor sport: whitewater canoeing. I signed up for a Swift Water Rescue Course in Ontario and spent that summer working as a canoe guide on rivers in the province of Quebec. Much as I liked guiding kids on weeklong canoe trips, I still experienced a pull toward rock climbing. I was not done exploring.

Again, having spent the first year of my five-year plan saving money, it was time for year 2, to go find my passion in the outdoors. Now that I had given canoeing a try for one summer, I was sure my future would have something to do with rock climbing. I had seen movies such as *Cliffhanger* and *Vertical Limits,* which depicted mountain guides jumping off cliffs, clinging to frozen ice or hanging off the edge of a rock like Tom Cruise in the opening scene of *Mission: Impossible II.* The life adventure these movies portrayed was becoming more and more appealing every day I spent outside and away from my windowless office in Toronto. I knew these movies were unrealistic portrayals of the mountain life, but the idea of becoming a mountain guide really appealed to me.

On a summer day in 2001 I had a very powerful session visualizing my 5-year intention around being physically strong, fit and active. I began having visions of very big mountains. These visions excited me because I was not just seeing the mountains from below, I was actually climbing up the side with lots of climbing gear attached and a big smile on my face. This energized me as I furiously wrote down the vision in my intentions journal, recording it to help inspire my next visualization session.

When engaging your intentions, there is a two-part process to ensure they become your reality. The first is to visualize. The second is to pay attention! Part 1 you have now done through Action Step 3. Part 2 is to start paying attention to what shows up in your life to help support your intentions. And here's an important secret: *everything* in your life is happening to support your intentions. If you begin to practise using this two-part

process with your intentions, you will notice things fitting into place in your life with more ease. With this comes renewed energy and ultimately better health. It is eye-opening when you first become aware of this reality. This is a very powerful secret that you now possess. Use it and pass it on to those who are ready to hear it.

ACTION STEP 5.
PAY ATTENTION TO YOUR INTENTIONS

I realized early on in my intention practice how important it was to pay attention to everything that showed up in my life. It was not always easy to make sense of it all, but through daily practice in paying attention to how everything played a role to help me achieve my intentions, I found I was able to make decisions more easily and powerful results started to appear. The following guidelines can help you pay more attention:

1. In your Power of Food Notebook, open to a blank page and list three people you talked to today. Leave four lines empty below each name. Perhaps these people included your mother, a co-worker or a stranger on the street.
2. Visualize each person in your mind one at a time and recall what your conversation was about.
3. Write down in the lines below each name some of the key points from your conversation.
4. Take a look at your list of 5-YEAR INTENTIONS and note where any of the key conversation points link with any one of your intentions.
5. In the next empty space available, list one action step you will take to follow up on that conversation point

that matched your intention. It happened for a reason and will lead you to more clarity toward achieving that intention.

6. Pay closer attention to each conversation you have today and how it fits in with one or more of your 5-YEAR INTENTIONS. Be sure to take action where you feel it helps expand you ability to attain any one of your intentions.

WHAT YOU CAN EXPECT: By practising this action step daily, you will become a master at paying attention. You will respond more quickly to the things around you throughout your day that support your intentions. You will become more efficient with your time and more organized as well. How many decisions do you make in a day? Are they often confusing to make or do they lead to frustration? When you get good at paying attention, decisions become easier to make because you begin to know which ones serve you and which ones do not, based on how they fit with your intentions.

As I said, in 2001 I had a very powerful vision while engaging my strong, fit and active intention in which I was on the side of a big mountain, climbing. With me climbing was someone whom I could not quite make out. It was invigorating to see myself climbing this way. At this point I was still struggling with old demons. I was living on a diet of mostly processed foods, battling with my weight issues and taking several medications— for asthma, high cholesterol and heartburn. I still experienced frequent anxiety attacks and was tired most of the time. I knew I was on the right track, but the renewed and strengthening Adam was only one year old, compared to the 26 years I'd been living under the old regime.

That same day I was sitting on my sofa watching TV, my number one activity at the time for numbing my mind and forgetting about my day, when the phone rang. I had received several phone calls from one of my good friends, Dave, over the previous two weeks. I was unable to get back to him, not because I was screening his calls, but because I was going through a bit of a setback with depression and did not feel comfortable speaking to anyone. When the phone rang and I saw the caller was Dave, I knew right away that it was him I had been climbing with during my earlier vision. I picked up the phone right away, knowing how important it was to pay attention to what showed up to support my intentions. Even though I did not know it yet, I was already getting better at paying attention to all the choices presented to me throughout my day, and Dave was holding a key piece to me fulfilling many of my 5-year intentions.

One moment I was picking up the phone and the next I was heading out the door to meet Dave for dinner. During our meal Dave began to share an opportunity I knew I had to take. He was heading off to Golden, BC, for another winter of ski guiding, and he invited me to join him. He knew I was looking for a change in life and felt strongly this would be a good move for me. I had been curious about British Columbia for some time, especially since I had begun to rock climb a few years earlier. Climbing that mountain with Dave during my visualization session sealed the deal for me, and I agreed to join him for a season in Golden.

That was in September 2001. Two months later I had boxed all my possessions, moved out of my apartment and said goodbye to all my family and friends. It was not the easiest thing to do, but for the sake of my health I made the move. On November 10, 2001, Dave and I hopped into my vw Jetta and hit the road. We spent the

Be open to the opportunities that are in front of you right now. The Universe is constantly aligning your dominant thoughts to receive and experience all you desire.

next four days driving across Canada, and after some 42 hours of driving, 4,500 kilometres away from home, arrived in Golden. This was to be my first of many winters spent exploring the spectacular mountains of BC.

A GLIMPSE INTO THE FUTURE

The first year of my five-year plan was for saving money to be able to leave the "rat race." My second year was spent exploring my passion for the outdoors through more rock climbing, whitewater canoeing and eventually moving to the mountains in Golden. The third year, I had planned to get efficient in my outdoor pursuits and begin exploring the industry for potential job opportunities. It was during year 3 of my five-year plan that I first met Isaac.

Isaac was only around 23 when we met. Also from Ontario, Isaac had discovered Whistler, BC, as a teenager and moved to Golden in search of a quieter scene. He was "living the life," spending his winters skiing big mountains and summers climbing and river rafting. Isaac was smaller than I was in stature, about 5'8", but on a set of telemark skis in the mountains, no one I knew could match him. I was truly impressed with his ability to ski some of the steepest, biggest and scariest lines in the Rocky Mountains and make it look easy. Isaac was not the only person I had come to know in Golden who was able to excel in the mountains without breaking much of a sweat.

Golden (pop. 4,200) is located some 260 kilometres west of Calgary, Alberta, and 700 kilometres east of Vancouver, BC. Yoho National Park, Banff National Park, Glacier National Park, Mount Revelstoke National Park and my favourite, Bugaboo Provincial Park, are all within a two-hour drive. Its proximity to all these parks makes Golden the ideal location for aspiring ski, climbing, alpine and all-around mountain guides. I quickly realized that an overweight, pre-diabetic guy from Toronto would have some trouble in the mountains keeping up with such seasoned athletes. Yet many of these aspiring guides quickly opened their doors and hearts to this unhealthy specimen so eager to learn and live. I spent my first winter and summer in Golden acclimatizing to my new surroundings and learning how to live and play in the mountains. My second winter and summer in Golden were when I took advantage of all the

opportunities before me and strengthened my hold on my new life.

I was now in year 3 of my five-year plan. I was spending a few minutes each morning practising visualizing my intentions, which had evolved and become clearer and more powerful. I developed my own system for engaging my intentions when I moved to Golden. I called it "My First Ten," a system that allowed me to heighten my daily visualization practice and also allowed me to share my practice more easily with others. I had begun to realize how the first few minutes of my day related to how the rest of my day played out. If I woke up feeling tired and grumpy, the rest of my day became filled with negative thoughts and poor results. If I woke up well rested and happy, my day was usually very productive and inspiring. "My First Ten" allowed me to wake up most

mornings feeling supercharged with energy and excited to start my day.

ACTION STEP 6.
PRACTISE "MY FIRST TEN"

I have been using "My First Ten," a system for engaging my intentions, for about 10 years now. It has given me direction, allowed me to overcome depression and enabled me to discover the power of food. How you spend the first 10 minutes of each day is your entrance point to creating a healthier, stronger, happier you. "My First Ten" is designed to heighten the power around your engagement with your intentions and set your energy for the day to positive.

I discovered the joy of cooking at the age of 29. Up until then I just ate.

1. After you get out of bed each morning, spend the first 10 minutes of your day engaging your intentions with meaning in a closed room that can be your daily practice space. If you do not have your own private room, use your closet or your bathroom. There is always somewhere you can practise.

2. During your 10 minutes, be aware of your surroundings and be as present as possible. At first this might be challenging, but it will get easier.

3. At the conclusion of your "My First Ten" practice, be aware of your thoughts as you continue on with your daily routine. Any time you are met with a challenge and your thoughts turn negative, take three deep breaths and place yourself back into your morning practice and connect to the positive feelings you were

experiencing then. This will reset your energy back to positive and help you move through your day with ease.

4. Every day, practise "My First Ten" after you get up.

WHAT YOU CAN EXPECT: "My First Ten" is a very powerful practice with the ability to fast-track all your desired results while allowing you to live each day abundantly happy and healthy. I promise, if you practice "My First Ten" on a daily basis, you will be witness to your own evolution, and it all starts with your first thought of each day. By spending a few moments first thing in the morning engaging positive thoughts around your intentions, you will shift your entire day's decisions to align with your intentions, making life flow with ease. Sound too easy to be true? Well, it *is* true. No pill to pop, no special diet to follow, just you and your thoughts: that's the key to true happiness and abundant health. Give it a try and see for yourself.

At the same time I introduced "My First Ten" into my life, I began to explore more with food. As you already know, I had been a processed-food junkie most of my life and spent very little time in the kitchen. As I got more active outside and began feeling more positive, I noticed myself spending more time in my kitchen. This was very new to me, for I had not enjoyed cooking before—up until I was 29 years old, I just ate.

My experimentation began with a few stir-fries and soups. The soups eventually turned into stews, and before I knew it I was making my own vegetable burgers and gourmet sandwiches to take into the mountains, full of fresh vegetables and the new hummus recipe I was so proud of (see Hungry Hungry Hummus, page 120).

Although this new enjoyment I was feeling in my kitchen came as a big surprise to me, I also knew it fit in very well with being strong, fit and active, which was one of my 5-year intentions. I was inspired to keep my new love for being in the kitchen going, and my friend Isaac played a very large role in what happened next.

During my second year in Golden, year 4 of my five-year plan, I moved in with Isaac. Of all my new family in Golden, Isaac was particularly inspirational. Having spent my first winter and summer in Golden discovering cooking and the joy of the stir-fry, I found that Isaac had a daily routine when it came to eating that baffled me. You see, Isaac was the first guy I had ever met whose kitchen cupboards were full of glass jars. Every day Isaac would open up a few of his jars and prepare amazing and tasty meals. These glass jars were full of different nuts and dried fruits, grains and seeds. This was a strange sight for someone who had grown up eating mainly cookies, chocolate bars, grilled cheese sandwiches and other processed foods. Once I began to incorporate a few of Isaac's strange foods into my diet, I began to experience profound changes to my health as well as in my ability to keep up in the mountains.

DISCOVERING

THE POWER

OF FOOD

THANKS TO THE NEW JOY I found in the kitchen and the inspiration of Isaac's cupboards, I spent much of year 4 of my five-year plan playing in the mountains and studying food while paying my way through the seasons as a server for a restaurant at the top of the ski hill. I was so inspired by my new lifestyle and heightened energy, I began researching each of my ailments one at a time. I was still on medication for high cholesterol, I occasionally experienced anxiety or a bout of depression, I was still 20 pounds overweight and daily heartburn was still an issue, but I was inspired to take further action to heal myself.

I spent countless hours studying from dozens of books and websites all about high cholesterol and the digestive system. This initial research led me to discover what I now call "The Big Three"—fats, proteins and carbohydrates. These macronutrients are the building blocks of all life, and I had taken them for granted my entire life. Understanding how fats, proteins and carbohydrates work for and against my health helped me begin to regain control over my own health without having to spend thousands of dollars relying on diets, cleanses, supplements and prescription drugs.

Wanting to thrive in the mountains, I continued to study how food worked and how my body used food to achieve my proper weight, abundant energy, increased strength, endurance and better all-round health. I would then spend countless hours in the kitchen creating meals from scratch with all the foods I was learning about, such as different types of grains, legumes, seeds and nuts as well as fruits and vegetables. Each day was spent learning, creating and playing.

ACTION STEP 7.
SAY HELLO TO YOUR GRANDMOTHER

After seeing Isaac's cupboards I quickly realized I had been missing something. On my next visit home to see my family, I called my grandmother and made a plan to visit her. I was not really surprised when I opened up her cupboards and saw row after row of glass jars filled with nuts, seeds, grains and legumes. After seeing that, I knew I was on the right track with my new exploration of food.

1. Call up your grandmother and tell her how much your love her. If your grandmother is no longer with us, visualize her for a moment and send some loving thoughts her way.

2. Now invite yourself over and take a look in her cupboards. If your grandmother is no longer with us, you'll need to modify this action step, perhaps with a close friend's support.

3. Take notice of what foods you see in your grandmother's cupboards.

WHAT YOU CAN EXPECT: If you are like me, you did not grow up eating food out of glass jars. My food came from a box, a can or a takeout container. This exercise will shed some light on how disconnected you may be from food. It also points to a possible gap in your food knowledge and opens up a big opportunity to begin exploring how you use food to live a healthy and energized life.

MY DAILY GOLDEN DIET

When I first moved to Golden my daily diet consisted of a large bowl of Frosted Flakes, followed by a peanut butter and jam sandwich for lunch, chocolate bars for snacks and a dinner that was usually a stir-fry. By the end of year 4 of my five-year plan, my days started with a bowl of homemade quinoa cereal or a smoothie with hemp milk, sesame seeds and goji berries. I would then head out for a day of hard climbing or big-mountain skiing with a packed lunch. Avocado, beet and tahini brown rice wraps, my homemade Power Date Bars (page 11) and my Mojo Power Snack Pack (page 56) provided me with ample energy throughout many high-mountain adventures. Most days would end by creating a new meal based on my most recent research or what I had discovered while watching the Food Network during a training session at the gym.

Yes, I was back at the gym working out, but this time it was fun, because there was purpose behind each session. I was training to increase my strength, fitness and endurance. I would then proceed to find friends to try my new kitchen creations. I was so proud of my recipes that sharing my discoveries and creations became an obsession. Common reactions from friends included: *Dude, where did you learn how to cook like that? Can you show me how to make this? It's awesome. Can I have the recipe?*

The positive reactions I received from friends motivated me even more. They kept me going in the kitchen, trying new and creative recipes to test in the mountains. Within two years I had transformed myself from being severely kitchen illiterate to having life-altering skills in the art of the power of food. By year 5 of my five-year plan I had taught myself which foods offered superior nutritional value for optimal health, how to use them in creative ways and how my body would use each nutrient to perform vital functions to keep my immune system strong and maintain abundant energy all day long. I was feeling so confident and proud of myself for taking action for my own health, and the results were impressive.

I was down to 170 pounds, 30 pounds less than when I had arrived in Golden. My cholesterol levels had returned to normal, allowing me to stop my medication. My depression was also losing its hold. I was so excited by my improved love of life and how food was becoming such an integral part of my healing process, I began calling my family and friends back home to share all my discoveries. I was the happiest I had ever been in my life, and I knew this feeling was only the beginning.

FINDING PURPOSE

I boarded the plane for a trip back to Toronto in April 2004 with an idea. I was going to introduce my whole family to the power of food. I had introduced my mother several months earlier to some of the new living foods I had discovered. As I told her then and still say now, there is no need to change your diet. Simply add a few of these key Power Foods, such as ground flaxseeds and hemp seeds, to your diet and you will begin to feel more energized. My mother's excitement at being able to manage her weight better as well as feel an increase in energy drove her to share her discoveries with her friends. Over the ensuing months I received a number of emails and phone calls from family and friends all wondering how they too could learn about the power of food.

Overwhelmed by the great response, I realized I had stumbled upon something spectacular. The power of food was something people needed and wanted. Food is one of the main contributors to our overall health, either positive or negative. I had experienced years of the negative impacts of eating the wrong foods and was only just beginning to understand food's positive powers.

As I mentioned earlier, after graduating from university, I had no idea what I was going to do with my life. Not until I wrote down what I wanted my life to look like five years from now did my life start to flow in a positive direction. It seems too easy, but this simple act of writing down my intentions had such tremendous power, especially because I engaged my intentions through a daily visualization practice. This practice led me to discover the power of food and to find my life's purpose. Days of feeling as if I were drowning from trying to swim up a river became less frequent. Now most days I feel as if I am flowing with the current, effortlessly, smoothly and with lots more energy.

Practising engaging my intentions over the past several years had given me everything I had visualized. I found a new life in Golden, where I was now strong, fit and active. I lived in a beautiful home with great friends, I was waking up each day energized and excited about life and I had discovered my purpose in life—to share the power of food. The beautiful, loving wife and children and successful business were on

their way. Mine was no longer a business focused on being in the outdoors, as I had first written down several years before. It was now a business based on sharing everything I had discovered about the power of food with as many people as I possibly could. This was my purpose in life. I knew it the moment I reconnected with food, and my passion for sharing the power of food continues to grow stronger every day.

~~~~~

At the age of 31, I found my life's purpose. Up until then I just lived.

PASSION INTO BUSINESS

In 2005 I made the tough decision to move away from Golden after four unforgettable years. Nine hours west by road was the city of Vancouver. Knowing I would need a bigger audience than Golden's for my message about the power of food, I moved 45 minutes north of Vancouver to the community of Squamish (pop. 17,158), which calls itself the "Outdoor Recreation Capital of Canada." Just like Golden, Squamish has access to some of the best outdoor recreation options in the world. Moving to Squamish not only put me closer to Vancouver's large urban population, but also gave me access right outside my front door to mountain biking, ski touring, kite boarding, trail running and some of the best rock climbing in all of North America.

My five-year plan was now at an end. I had saved up enough money to leave work and explore my options, I had begun playing outside and testing my skills, I had moved across the country and boosted my strength, I had developed inspiring new habits to elevate my health, I had

discovered the power of food along with my purpose in life and I was now on track to begin turning my passion into a business.

After arriving in Squamish I quickly set up a space where I could practise "My First Ten." I allowed my daily practice visualizing my intentions to continue to guide me toward my next move. I developed my vision for a business called Power of Food while implementing ways to bring my knowledge to the world. Starting a business from scratch was a lot more challenging then I could have ever imagined. No amount of business school education can prepare you for getting out on your own and making it a success. Thank goodness I had discipline with my daily practice visualizing my intentions plus unlimited passion, abundant energy and the power of food to help keep me going through the process.

It has been almost 10 years since I founded Power of Food, a company that prides itself on sharing easy strategies for living your life abundantly happy and healthy. The business brings purpose to my life and continues to nourish my soul on the deepest levels. It has also reached thousands of people just like you in very powerful ways. From dozens of personal coaching clients to members of non-profit organizations and large corporations, Power of Food has touched many lives. I am humbled every time I walk into an organization and get a chance to meet so many wonderful people who share their daily struggles with me. I see myself in every set of eyes I connect with and feel honoured to share in this very powerful exchange in energy.

As my intentions continue to evolve, I become more and more confident that we all have access to the unlimited potential within for living a life of purpose. Writing down my 5-year intentions, visualizing daily though "My First Ten," allowing the healing power of nature to become a part of my life and discovering the power of food: together these have given me power to live a life I never knew possible. Twelve years ago I was at rock bottom and a mess—pre-diabetic, depressed, overweight and filled with self-pity and a sense of unworthiness. Today I am fit, strong, energized and confident, and I love myself more and more with each moment. If you wake up every single morning feeling abundantly happy and healthy, you are already there. If you want this for yourself or for someone you love, I am happy to now share with you what I discovered about the power of food. Along with engaging your intentions on a daily basis and spending time with nature, the power of food is your key to unlocking your greatness and will have you living the most powerful life imaginable.

ACTION STEP 8.
STRENGTHEN YOUR VISION

I have made several vision boards over the past 10 years. Each one highlights a very specific time in my life and holds tremendous power. When I hold them side by side, it is like looking at a massive storyboard of how the last dozen years of my life have unfolded. I use my vision boards to heighten my energy around my intentions and create more clarity on what I want. They are a key component of my daily "My First Ten" practice and contribute to the ease with which I achieve my results.

Seeing something before your eyes can be very powerful. With a vision board you are taking your desires and bringing them into the material world. Creating a vision board helps put attention, energy and focus on your intentions and serves as a powerful reminder of what lies just around the corner if you want it. Clarity is important in order to achieve your intentions. Vision boards help you become clearer on your intentions. Here's how to create your very own vision board:

1. First thing to do is get organized. Find a box and place all your supplies into it: markers, tape, glue stick, scissors, stickers and any other items you would like to use in creating your vision board.

2. Go to your local dollar store and purchase a poster board or canvas. Think of your "My First Ten" practice space. Then pick a size of canvas or board that will fit your space.

3. Gather and look through old magazines, newspapers and catalogues for photos and inspiring words that represent what you desire. The Internet also presents a wealth of possibilities for your vision board; friends and family might also have old magazines to rummage through.

4. Cut out pictures, words and images that represent your 5-YEAR INTENTIONS. When choosing items, think about where you would like to see your life in six months, two years or five years from now. Also consider what your mind created for your eyes to see during your last visualization session.

5. Create one vision board for all your intentions or make a separate vision board for each of your intentions. I have one for my business, one for my home, one for my garden, one for my family life and another focusing on my outdoor sports. Feel free to go as grand as you can making your vision board, and don't worry if it does not look *exactly* as you desire. I have created several vision boards, and they always evolve as I achieve my intentions and set new ones.

6. Choose a special location for your vision board. Your "My First Ten" daily practice space is the ideal location to hang your vision board. You may also wish to place your vision board in another location. It is up to you where you put your vision boards, but it is important you make them a part of your daily practice. I even have a few clients who take pictures of their vision boards with their phones so they can engage them while travelling.

7. Reward your eyes. When you have hung your vision board it is now a part of you. Take as little as 30 seconds during your "My First Ten" practice and dive into your creation. What do you see in front of you? What have you put attention, energy and focus toward? If it is on your vision board, you can experience it before you eyes.

8. Add one or two pictures each week until your vision board feels complete.

WHAT YOU CAN EXPECT: Do you like your results to come fast? Do you like them to come with ease? Creating a vision board is one great way to help increase your chances of seeing every result you want in life. The more time you spend focusing on your vision board as described in this action step, the more you will see the items on your board manifest before your eyes. This book is proof of the power of vision boards: *The Power of Food* book has been a vision board of mine for some time and one I have focused on during my "My First Ten" practice for a few years.

ADAM'S 5-YEAR INTENTIONS MANIFESTED

If you recall, I shared with you my 5-year intentions earlier in *The Power of Food*. Here are those intentions once again.

- To live in a beautiful home
- To have a loving wife and children
- To be physically strong, active and fit
- To wake up energized and excited about life
- To have a successful business related to being outdoors

If you follow the 12 action steps described throughout *The Power of Food*, you will begin to manifest all your intentions right before your eyes. I am living proof of the power of following these steps.

You miss 100 percent of the shots you don't take. —Wayne Gretzky

SECOND-GENERATION FAST-FOOD EATERS

Whatever happened to all those glass jars full of nuts, seeds, grains and legumes that filled our parents', grandparents' or great-grandparents' kitchen cupboards or pantry? I did not realize before moving in with Isaac in Golden how detached I really was in my relationship to food. Standing in front of my grandmother's kitchen cupboards many years ago, I realized my own family and many others had lost a style of eating that for generations had kept humans strong and healthy. During the past 60 years many of us gradually lost our awareness of the importance of food and how powerful nutrition is for maintaining optimal health. Our overdependence on fast and convenient foods has led many North Americans into a state of obesity and diabetes. Poor food choices in turn lead to an inability to manage our daily stress, which causes internal inflammation, resulting in unnecessary illness and disease. I call this the "Second-Generation Fast-Food Eater" syndrome.

We in North America are living in unprecedented times as far as both the poor quality of foods we eat and our unhealthy conditions. One of the most popular fast-food restaurants first opened its doors in the early 1950s, in California, and at the same time consumers were introduced to the first frozen meals designed to eat at home. Frozen TV dinners gained popularity very quickly and the fast-food craze took off, to the point where many households in North America began experiencing a shift in their relationship to food.

When you google statistics on obesity or diabetes, you discover there is a direct correlation between the rise of obesity and diabetes and the increased availability of processed foods in North America. Why did processed foods become so popular so fast? They are cheap; they satisfy our taste buds; they please the eye; and they are available everywhere. The convenience of processed foods and our lack of awareness about their damaging health effects are two major reasons for the decline of North Americans' health over the past 60 years.

The baby boomer generation, now in their fifties and sixties, were, for the most part, the first generation to feed their children fast, overprocessed food. Before the baby boomer generation, processed food did not exist to the extent it exploded in the late 1960s, '70s and '80s. By the early 1980s and into the 1990s, processed food had become a major convenience for baby boomers as they struggled to juggle family life and aging parents. After the baby boomers came Generation X, now in their thirties and forties. Generation X started feeding their children processed foods from a young age. Many members of Generation X, like myself, grew up on processed food and were never educated about healthy eating, either at school or at home. During the same time there was a large growth in big-box grocery stores, which led to a further disconnect from local and living foods. Both the baby boomers and Generation Xers were choosing to eat and choosing to feed their loved ones nutrient-deficient food.

Over the generations, as North Americans continued to embrace processed foods and all their perceived benefits, along came a third generation of processed-food eaters, Generation Y, next in line to inherit our addiction to processed foods. This generation not only consumed processed foods at alarming rates, but also began feeding their kids, the so-called Generation Z (also known as the Internet Generation), the same unhealthy foods, leading to a sharp rise in obesity and diabetes among children.

Today many of our friends, family members, co-workers, children and others struggle to feel well and are challenged to maintain a level of energy to get them through their day. Whether it is cancer, heart disease, diabetes or obesity, many of our current health conditions have their roots in our unhealthy relationship to food. Why should it be surprising, then, to see so many North American adults and children relying on diets, supplements, cleanses, vitamins and pharmaceuticals to help alleviate their individual ailments? Myself, I spent thousands of dollars on protein shakes and prescription drugs, the newest fad diet and the latest brand of vitamin, all to help treat my poor health. The majority of these options only caused me to feel worse. Every diet I ever tried ended in failure and led me to feel more guilty, frustrated and angry. These negative feelings always reached their peak when I eventually gained back all the weight I had lost—and more—after a diet. Does this scenario apply to you or someone you know?

Like many others looking to get healthy, I did not know what to do or where to begin. There was no solution I had tried that had helped me to experience any long-term weight loss, benefit from more sustained energy or get off of my prescription drugs. Nothing I ever did to get healthy was based on repair and prevention. I was always choosing band-aid solutions, which only covered up my symptoms for a short period of time. Essentially my body was in a constant state of dis-ease. My daily medications only masked my underlying health problems. My body was lacking vital nutrients due to my processed-food diet, and my mind was suffering because of my unhappy thoughts.

Our fast-paced lives and disconnect from food has led many baby boomers, Generation Xers, Generation Y young adults and now many Generation Z children into a state of confusion around how to prevent or cure the dis-ease in their bodies and minds. One thing we have become very good at is grasping for the next one-of-a-kind, quick-fix solution. Alas, most of these "solutions" only mask our conditions and do nothing to reconnect us to our own health. Luckily there is a better way, and it is not difficult.

NOT ANOTHER DIET!

Many of my Power of Food coaching clients have mentioned to me how the word "diet" brings up heavy emotions. As it did for me, this word may be associated with much trauma in your life. I acknowledge your pain, and I also want to explore the reasons behind it. Why is it that North American consumers have been subjected to countless diets since the mid-1950s? What makes us all so different that we need to have multiple diets, all promising to release us from our feelings of guilt, anger and frustration through the improvement of our weight or diabetic states?

Now, I don't want to get too political here, but diets are a multi-billion-dollar business. They represent supply and demand at its most basic form. The demand is at an all-time high and is only getting higher as obesity and diabetes reach epidemic proportions. With the rise in demand we see a rise in supply. If you take a look at the history of diets, you can see that as obesity has increased through the years, so has the number of different types of diets being offered. It is this basic law of supply and demand that has driven the diet industry for decades. Bombarded by countless claims of salvation, North Americans get to choose their next diet as if they were choosing a new flavour of ice cream. The diet you choose may help you feel better about yourself for a little while, but in the end most diets lead only to failure.

The issue lies within the concept of diets. Defined as a regulated selection of food, diets do not set you up for long-term success. As a one-dimensional solution, diets do nothing to get at the roots of why you do what you do, why you take the daily actions you take. They only leave you back at square one with a lighter wallet and feelings of frustration and guilt. And by restricting you from something, diets also cause conflict. To experience abundant health and happiness, you must stop reaching for solutions that restrict you in any way and begin looking at what you can start bringing into your life, representing acts of love. Engaging your intentions is a very powerful daily act of love. Eating living food is another very powerful act of love. Both can be achieved without restricting your life in any way and have profound positive effects on your mind and body. The more you add in, the happier, stronger and more energized you will become.

Let food be your medicine and medicine be your food. —Hippocrates

WHY THE BIG SECRET ABOUT FOOD?

Did you know that there are over 300,000 choices of food to select from in North America? Even more alarming is the fact that depending on which grocery store you visit, you may find 30,000 to 60,000 choices *in that store alone*. That's a lot of choice.

Do you find it confusing walking through your local grocery store? Eating healthy food does not have to be confusing! The desire for a healthier diet has gained momentum over the past decade due to so many people feeling unwell. Do you suffer from daily fatigue? Do you still feel tired when you wake up in the morning? How about sugar or carbohydrates: do you crave them often? How do your joints or muscles feel? Are they a little stiff or sore? With so much confusion surrounding the foods we eat and whether they are healthy or not, many of us resort to one-dimensional solutions such as diets, supplements and cleanses to find relief. There has never been a better time to get back to basics to begin healing what ails you from the inside out.

How would you feel if you could walk into your grocery store and know exactly what the ideal foods are to feed yourself and your family for abundant energy and to help stop your food cravings? This is one of the most empowering experiences possible and strengthens your passion for life in ways you never knew existed. There is one big secret around food that will help make your next grocery store visit more empowering as you begin to discover how to eat for abundant health and happiness: *there are only two kinds of food.* That's it.

This big secret I have just shared with you is the key to cutting out any confusion you may have around food. So what are the two kinds of food? I ask this question during each of my Power of Food live events, and 99% of the time I hear back from the audience: "Good and bad." Yes, "good and bad" is fairly accurate, but I like to call these two food types by different names. The food you choose to eat is either living food or processed food. Living food is food that grows on trees or in the ground. Processed food is food that has very little nutritional value. You are either eating food that is alive or you are eating food that is processed and partially or completely dead.

THE LIVING FOOD REVOLUTION

After spending several years researching nutrition during my time in Golden, I came to realize one very important fact. No matter what you read in the newspaper or online, no matter what your co-workers are talking about at the office, your ability to get healthier all comes down to eating more living foods than processed foods.

Living foods are any foods that have not been broken down, altered or transformed in any way. Living foods exist in their complete state and offer superior nutritional value when compared to processed foods.

Mindful of delivering information that is accessible, I am happy to tell you there are only six living foods you need to know about. Once you know these six foods you are good to go! *Only six?* you ask. *How is that possible, Adam?* Well, the truth is there are only six *food groups* to discover. I call these the Power of Food Groups. These six Power of Food Groups are based on living foods that, when included as a part of your daily diet, have the ability to help you begin to heal your body and mind from illness and disease. These Power of Food Groups all come from the soil beneath your feet and the living plants and trees that surround you. In no particular order they are nuts, seeds, grains, legumes, fruits and vegetables.

These foods may all sound familiar to you, and they may even be a large part of your diet already. I told you this was not going to be complicated. Many of these foods you already have in your kitchen. But unfortunately, in North America most people's diets include a large amount of meat and dairy products as well as overprocessed foods, depleted of their nutritional qualities.

I am not asking you to eliminate meat, dairy products or processed foods from your diet. As I already mentioned, "no restrictions" is the key to seeing the healthy results you desire. What you *add* to your current daily diet will provide the nutrients you need to thrive while reconnecting you to food. As you begin adding in the good, which also represents a very big act of love for yourself, you will find it easier and easier to start removing the bad. That might sound too good to be true. However, it worked for me and has worked for thousands of others who have ditched the diets and begun adding in some very powerful living foods on a daily basis.

~~~~~~~~

It is time to stop trying to remove the darkness from your life and start bringing in some very powerful sources of light. Let food be that light.

SPEND A DAY WITH A FARMER

Now that you have a better understanding of the power of living foods, I want to take you behind the scenes to look at one important aspect of the commercialized food industry. This is to help shed some light on the difference between living foods and processed foods. Let me ask you a question: in North America, what is the number one ingredient your friends and family eat on a daily basis? If you said "wheat" you would be correct.

Now let's take a quick look at a typical North American farmer. A wheat farmer has his fields of wheat. The wheat is in its whole, living state. It has not been broken down, altered or transformed in any way and contains lots of protein, great fibre and complex carbohydrates. In order to make money and survive, the farmer must harvest the wheat and ship it out for production. Once harvested, the wheat grain is sent to be milled. During the milling process the wheat is broken down, mainly using heat, destroying much of its nutritional value. In modern agriculture, using heat is the most efficient way to process a grain into flour, and the quicker the process, the bigger the profit. A few options exist that are less destructive when processing

grains, such as stone grinding or steel cutting, but the majority of commercial wheat flour in North America is made using a heat process. And this heat-processed flour is the main ingredient in most processed-food products.

Take a moment and visualize all the different foods you eat made from wheat. Did you have any bread in the past few days? How about crackers, pizza, cereals, cookies or pasta—did they find their way into your diet lately? With very little nutritional value, processed food provides you with only empty calories; it leaves you starving for energy while at the same time it pads your waistline.

Do you find yourself craving sugar before noon? How about carbohydrates for dinner? I used to be known around my office as the chocolate guy. My office drawer was like a vending machine full of chocolate bars. Each bite gave me a quick burst of energy, but later I would always experience an equivalent energy crash that would send me back to my desk drawer for another hit. Do you know a chocolate guy or girl in your office, home or school? Is it you perhaps?

If you are struggling to stay awake throughout your day or wondering how to lose those dreaded extra 10, 20 or 30 pounds, it is time to start looking at the foods you are *not* eating. As you probably understand by now, feeling more sustained energy throughout your day is not about eliminating the chocolate, cookies, crackers or cake. If you really want more energy and a slimmer waistline, you must start to add living foods into your diet. Before I share all my secrets on how to begin adding in the good while still eating the bad, let me first finish up the story of our typical North American farmer.

As mentioned earlier, by the time it gets to your mouth, wheat flour contains very little nutritional value. So what about the taste? What do you suppose flour tastes like? When was the last time you tried eating flour? Not too tasty, right? So in order to make processed wheat products—the bread, crackers, cereal or cookies—taste good, food manufacturers pump each product full of additives. And—surprise, surprise—the three ingredients most North Americans become addicted to from a young age happen to also be the top three ingredients food manufacturers add to processed foods to ensure you will want to eat them: salt, sugar and fat.

TASTE-BUD BLUES

Nearly from the minute we are born, most North Americans are introduced to salt, sugar and fat. Right after the processed grains—mostly wheat, corn and rice—salt, sugar and fat are the three most common additives in commercially processed foods. And, as I've already outlined, these processed foods make up the majority of our diets. Salt, sugar and fat also happen to be three of the most damaging food additives to our health, linked to ADHD and food allergies, obesity and diabetes as well as heart disease and high blood pressure. Salt, sugar and fat have overtaken our grocery store shelves like a virus, and our taste buds have been taken hostage because these additives hook us to these processed foods, causing an addiction many have little control over. And our food addiction leads to very big profits for food manufacturers.

Our taste buds are constantly searching for salt, sugar and fat every time we eat something. And unless we feed our addiction, our taste buds will fight back and begin a chemical process leading to a rise in cortisol, "the stress hormone," which often leads to a craving for more carbohydrates. This is a vicious cycle indeed. At the same time we experience a rise in cortisol, our taste buds send a pain or pleasure signal to our brain, informing us whether or not to be happy. In this way our taste buds

sabotage our ability to eat healthier foods.

For example, compared to salty, sugary, fatty processed foods, when you think about eating living foods, what comes to mind? Perhaps you think: *It won't taste good. Everything is going to be bland. There is no way my children will eat this stuff.* Do any of these thoughts come up for you? Our mind will do anything to avoid pain and anything to gain pleasure. Eating salty, sugary and fatty foods equals pleasure for the addict.

Two steps are required to release you from your food addiction and give you some space to begin your healing process. Step 1: Learn about some of the key foods within the six Power of Food Groups and start adding them to your diet immediately to help control your blood sugar. Step 2: Be mindful of how your taste buds are regulating your food addiction. Do not be too quick to dismiss a new healthy living food you are trying to add to your diet. Living foods will not give you the same rush of salt, sugar and fat as processed foods. As negative thoughts come up, take a moment to be aware of them and tell yourself you are adding this living, nutrient-rich food into your life to nourish your body and mind.

By practising these two steps every day, you will naturally detox your body and mind, allowing for new and healthy food habits to take over. Your new food habits will in turn lead to you feeling more energized, excited about life and one step closer to living your life of purpose. Flushing the years of toxic waste from your body and mind are two powerful results you will enjoy by adding in living foods while being mindful of your thoughts. As you wean your taste buds off their salt, sugar and fat dependency, your food addiction will lose its hold over you. Happier thoughts and a stronger body are waiting for you, and you still get to eat your cake!

LIVING FOODS FOR LIFE

If you still have questions about living foods and why they are so beneficial to health, here is yet more information. Living foods contain all their life-giving force built up by Mother Nature. They are, remember, grown on trees or in the ground. They are not pumped full of synthetic hormones, they are not fed a large dose of antibiotics and they contain superior nutritional qualities to processed foods. Every day your body needs essential fatty acids, complete proteins and complex carbohydrates along with key vitamins and minerals to survive. Further, the health of your immune system relies on the strength of your digestive system. It's a sad fact that most of our digestive systems are in distress. You know this if you suffer from constipation, bloating, excessive gas, irritable bowel syndrome, constant fatigue, daily food comas from overeating, or other digestive problems.

Living foods in the form of nuts, seeds, grains, legumes, fruits and vegetables—the six Power of Food Groups—when eaten daily, provide your body and mind with key nutrients required for optimal health in forms that are easier for the body to digest. Each of the six Power of Food Groups contains some special living foods. I call these the Power Foods and describe them in the recipe section. In total, two dozen sidebars highlight what makes these particular living foods so important to the health of your body and mind. You will discover the power of hemp seeds, goji berries, coconut and many more. Each living food heals from the inside and allows you to live each day more energized and stress free.

You may be thinking: *This is great, Adam. I now understand more about processed foods and the importance of living foods, but where do meat and dairy fit into the Power of Food?* I grew up eating mostly meat and dairy products at every meal. Does this sound familiar? I was told right from a young age that I needed my protein from meat and calcium from dairy. And I did not question this for more than 25 years, until I discovered the power of food. Let me first state: I still eat meat and dairy. However, I do so more rarely, and I am always aware of where my meat comes from. Even with all the antibiotics, hormones and genetically modified feed, meat and dairy have never been more popular in the North American diet. In the past I would often wonder where my protein was coming from if I did not have a piece of meat on my plate. I am happy to say those days are gone. Discovering the power of food allowed me to overcome my dependence on meat and dairy as my main source of protein. Having now lived on a diet consisting of 80% nuts, seeds, grains, legumes, fruits and vegetables for many years, I can honestly say I feel lighter, stronger, faster, fitter and more energized than I did when eating meat daily. I also no longer get the three or four colds or the flu every year that I once did.

Clients often tell me how they understand my position on meat and dairy but still believe these foods belong in their diet. I have heard this dozens and dozens of times, especially from male clients. I understand this viewpoint, because I used to be that guy. For years I played hockey (still do), and after each game the boys and I would go for burgers and beer. Such meals were part of my identity. After all, how can you go out with the guys and order carrot and celery sticks? However, such abstinence is not what I am talking about here. It is okay to believe you need to eat meat to survive, but if you are not feeling well, I encourage you to explore the power of living foods before your poor health forces you into early hockey retirement.

To reiterate, I am not telling you to stop eating meat or dairy products. In my case, I never forced myself to stop eating meat or dairy. This just happened on its own the more I ate living foods. What I found through eating more living foods was that the more I ate these healthier plant-based sources of protein, calcium and iron, the stronger my body and mind became. I became lean, fit and fast both in my thoughts and in my sports. I also began craving more of the living foods and less and less meat and dairy.

This is still one of the more exciting discoveries I am happy to share with you. Your body lives off of "The Big Three": fats, proteins and carbohydrates. Without these macronutrients you will die. If you feed your body one dominant source for these key nutrients, then that is what it will crave most. I never knew protein existed in nuts, seeds, grains, legumes, fruits and vegetables. But of course it does, as well as ample amounts of calcium and iron. Not only do living foods contain key vitamins, nutrients and minerals, they are also easier to digest, which gives you more energy and a stronger immune system. And who doesn't want that? So again, I am not telling you not to eat meat or dairy, but to start adding some living foods to your diet to help counteract any negative effects your current diet may be producing. By adding some Power Foods to your daily diet, you will begin to reduce your overdependence on meat and dairy for some of your key nutrients and allow living foods to nourish your body instead.

Reducing my meat and dairy consumption from daily to once every few months also allowed me to eliminate another one of my daily medications. For five or six years I relied on antacid medication to soothe the burning in my esophagus. Through my nutrition research I discovered where my heartburn was coming from. It was being caused by an excessive amount of protein in my system. My years of heavy meat and dairy consumption had caused a large amount of acid to build up in my digestive system. This caused inflammation and several other symptoms, such as higher cholesterol, fatigue, restless sleep and excessive heartburn. Once my body began to crave living food sources of protein that were much easier to digest—such as hemp seeds, goji berries and quinoa—I reduced my meat intake and my heartburn began to disappear almost immediately. Had I continued to mask my symptoms with antacid medication and continued to eat the same unhealthy foods, I'm sure I would have been diabetic or suffering from heart disease years ago.

I share this with you to help inspire you to be open to what your body is looking for to heal itself. My body and mind became more powerful then I ever could have imagined thanks to living food. The transformation started when I stopped masking my symptoms and began empowering myself through a strong desire to feel better. Your days of being confused around food, of grabbing the convenient, tasty and inexpensive option, are over. Your cravings for meat and dairy will soon subside, so you can make clear choices about what is best for your health and happiness. Get ready to say goodbye to your processed-food addiction and enjoy heightened energy. It is time to get you on track with the Power of Food system I implemented many years ago, which helped me conquer the addictive hold of unhealthy foods over my life. It is called the 80/20 rule.

THE 80/20 RULE REVEALED

Take 30 seconds and imagine you are stranded on a desert island. Think of the one favourite food you would most like to have with you. I know for me it is, without a doubt, hemp seeds. Not too long ago I would have said shortbread cookies, but now it is hemp seeds. To think about your favourite food is to acknowledge the foods you love to eat and celebrate them. Living a healthy and happy life, as I have said, has nothing to do with restrictions or eliminating anything from your life or diet. It has everything to do with celebrating the foods you love while at the same time bringing in living foods that offer abundant nutritional value to help counter the impact of processed foods. That is where the 80/20 rule of eating comes in.

I was able to finally eliminate my addiction to processed food and to lose weight after I created a customized system for taking action. I called it the Power of Food 80/20 rule. Now, the 80/20 rule has been used in other scenarios, such as in business, where it means that 80% of your sales come from 20% of your clients. I created the Power of Food 80/20 rule to help me track the amount of living foods I eat every day. The ultimate daily goal is for 80% of my diet to come from within the six Power of Food Groups. This ensures I receive superior nutritional value in the form of living foods every single day. The other 20% of my diet can be any food I want, when I want, *no restrictions!*

In North America our main problem with the 80/20 rule is that we have it backwards! Eighty percent of what many North Americans eat on a daily basis are heavily processed foods, keeping us tired and hungry, and excessive meat and dairy, leaving our digestive systems in chaos. With our digestive systems constantly in distress due to our lack of nutrient-rich foods and our consumption of hard-to-digest meat and dairy, the 20% of what living foods we do eat are not being absorbed properly. At the same time, our immune systems shift vital energy away from fighting disease and illness to helping support our digestive process. This lack of nutrient absorption and shifting of energy for digestion leaves you vulnerable to more sickness and disease due to the weakening of your immune system.

If I told you starting today that 80% of your diet must come from the six Power of Food Groups—nuts, seeds, grains, legumes, fruits and vegetables—how would you feel? If you felt frustrated or confused as to where to begin, you would not be alone. Many of my clients have mentioned that 80% is too daunting. *I don't know where to begin. How is that possible? That won't be very much fun.* The great news is you do not need to be at 80% right now. Through my own success and based on the results of many of my Power of Food coaching clients, I know it is easiest to experience success, gain momentum and see results when starting with a smaller number. Smaller steps lead to bigger results over time, and 80% is attainable for everyone, but only after the Magic Number has been reached.

MAKING IT A LIFESTYLE WITH THE MAGIC NUMBER

The Magic Number to the Power of Food 80/20 rule, making it easier to experience daily success, is 51%. This is your starting point, not 80%. The key is to get to the point where you eat 51% of your daily diet based on living foods. Think of it in terms of trying to swim upriver. If you are constantly trying to swim upriver, eventually you will get tired and may give up. It is just a matter of time. At 51% you begin to get your head above water and feel what it is like to stop fighting against the current. This starts a shift in your daily routine until you realize you are now floating easily *down* the river. Can you imagine how you will feel when you reach 80%? You will, and you will be amazed at the difference.

Once your diet reaches 51% living foods, your body and mind begin to assist you in your daily ability to make change and take bigger action to support your new strength and energy. At this point you will begin experiencing a renewed sense of purpose. Your love of life will gain power as your new healthy lifestyle takes hold. And at this point 80% starts to happen on its own. Waking up ready to attack your day full of strength and energy is a very addictive feeling. It's a much nicer addiction then the old salt, sugar and fat dependency that once ran my life. You are not too far from reaching 80% consumption of living foods. It happens very quickly, but first you must reach the Magic Number of 51%.

FIVE STEPS TO MAGIC NUMBER SUCCESS

As you now know, I love to share my action steps to help ease you along your supercharged journey. You also know I am mindful of making things as accessible and achievable as possible. That is why I have broken down reaching the Magic Number into a five-step process. This five-step process will guide you to achieving the Magic Number of 51% with ease.

1.   Discover four to six key Power Foods within the six Power of Food Groups that you can start adding to your diet to reach your daily 51% consumption of living foods.

2.   Eat your four to six Power Foods as a healthy snack throughout your day.

3.   Begin to add each of the four to six Power Foods into your daily diet, without any restrictions on what else you eat.

4.   Get creative with your four to six Power Foods. Try making something from the recipe section.

5.   Track your success daily in your Power of Food *Daily Food Journal*. You'll find more information on using this journal and an example on page 41.

Let's take a closer look at each of these 5 steps.

1. DISCOVER THE POWER FOODS

As I have discussed in detail, the Power Foods are based on living foods that have not been broken down, altered or transformed in any way. They are superior in nutritional value and, when consumed, will keep you energized and feeling strong. Sidebars in the recipe section highlight 24 Power Foods (four in each of the six Power of Food Groups) that were important in my own evolution to a healthier mind and body.

There are four things to consider when choosing your four to six Power Foods. First, each food should be easy to find. The Power Foods highlighted in the recipe section are all just that. Second, each food must be easy to eat as a snack. Third, each food must be easy to add. This is not the case with all the Power Foods I highlight. For example, kale is high on my list of Power Foods, but I don't think you want to add kale to your morning cereal or oatmeal. (Pay special, close attention to nuts and seeds as your starting Power Foods to reach your daily 51%. They are easy to find, easy to eat as a snack and very easy to add without restricting your diet, and they taste great.) Fourth, each food should have the ability to help control your blood sugar. Controlling your blood sugar is important to staying committed when first starting to incorporate more living foods.

By adding Power Foods rich in quality proteins, essential fatty acids and complex carbohydrates, you will feel more energized throughout your day while experiencing fewer sugar cravings and more control of your food addictions. These Power Foods also begin to create a little more space between how you feel in a given situation and what action you take next. In other words, you become less reactionary and more proactive, making food decisions that serve your higher intentions.

It is now time to choose your four to six Power Foods

to start adding to your daily diet. Here are the six Power Foods I started with: hemp seeds, ground flaxseeds, chia seeds, almonds, goji berries and shredded coconut.

ACTION STEP 9.
PICK YOUR POWER FOODS

I started adding the six Power Foods mentioned above without restricting what I ate. I would make a week's worth of a living food trail mix containing all six ingredients. I would then go out to eat chili on my lunch break and add in 1 tbsp (15 mL) of my mix. If I ordered in pizza for dinner I would add 2 tbsp (30 mL) over the top of every slice I ate. If I made a turkey wrap or roast beef sandwich, I added 2 tbsp (30 mL) of my Power Foods mix. Very quickly I started to eat less and eventually began craving more of the good and less of the bad. Here's a process you can use to pick your own Power Foods.

1. Take a look at the 24 Power Foods featured in the recipe section.

2. List the top four to six Power Foods you will start adding to your diet tomorrow.

3. Go out and buy a one-month supply of your chosen Power Foods.

4. Place a small amount of each of your chosen Power Foods into a small glass jar and store it in the door of the refrigerator for easy access.

5. Place your remaining Power Foods in the freezer to keep them fresh.

6. To an airtight container, add ½ cup (125 mL) of each of your chosen Power Foods to create your own mix. Take this on the road to eat as a snack and easily add to everything you eat.

7. When on the road, eat 1 to 2 tbsp (15 to 30 mL) as desired to help control your blood sugar and reduce food cravings. Also add 1 to 2 tbsp (15 to 30 mL) of your mix to everything you eat throughout your day.

8. Keep a running count of how you are doing with the Magic Number through your Power of Food *Daily Food Journal*. Find more instructions on using the journal and sample entries on page 41.

9. Refill your Power Foods mix container at the end of each day to have enough for the following day.

WHAT YOU CAN EXPECT: Every time you add living foods to your diet, you give yourself a powerful act of love. These acts of love add up and bring some profound results. Within days you will begin feeling a steadier stream of energy while also enjoying some calmer moments and less stress. This in turn decreases internal inflammation, leading to weight loss and more vibrant skin, hair and eyes.

2. EAT YOUR CHOSEN POWER FOODS AS A SNACK

As described in Action Step 9, every day take with you on the road a container with a mix of your Power Foods to enjoy as a snack. As little as 1 tbsp (15 mL) of your mix will help control your blood sugar and begin giving you sustained energy. Within days you can expect to see a reduction in your food cravings; your addiction to sugar and carbohydrates becomes more manageable. As long as you eat 1 to 2 tbsp (15 to 30 mL) of your Power Foods mix several times throughout each day, you will feel some encouraging results very quickly. Be sure to always have a good stock of your Power Foods on hand to ensure you never go without them. Eating 4 to 6 tbsp (60 to 75 mL) a day is ideal and more is even better. *But Adam, can't I overdose on eating these foods?* Most of us are starving for nutrients and lack sufficient vitamins and minerals for optimal health. With our diets so reliant on processed foods and meat and dairy, you need to eat as much living food as you possibly can. You will not overdose on living foods. Just keep eating them and begin to notice how great you start to feel.

3. BEGIN TO ADD YOUR POWER FOODS

Step 3 to reaching the Magic Number of 51% is to start adding your chosen Power Foods into your daily diet without any restrictions on what you eat. This is the crucial stage where you simply add more nuts, seeds, grains, legumes, fruits and vegetables into your current diet to increase your nutritional intake while continuing to eat the foods you like. This is not a diet. It is a lifestyle, and by adding in the good, you will gain the opportunity to start removing the bad. I know that might sound a little strange, but it works. The more you add in the good, the easier it will become to start removing the bad from your life. If you start by trying to eliminate the bad, such as every diet I have ever tried, this only brings more bad in the form of stronger food cravings and feelings of frustration. It's time to turn this around and feel what it is like to truly experience success over and over again.

A gentleman attending a Power of Food live event once asked me: *So, Adam, what you are telling me is if I add hemp seeds to my Big Mac I will be healthier?* The answer is *yes*. Hemp seeds have great nutritional value, a Big Mac, not so much. The main thing you get from a Big Mac is useless calories, so of course the answer is yes. Start adding your Power Foods to everything you eat beginning tomorrow morning.

4. GET CREATIVE WITH YOUR POWER FOODS

Step 4 is all about taking your Power Foods to the next level. By getting creative using the six Power of Food Groups, you will begin to see a steady increase in your daily consumption of living foods. Here is where you strengthen your love, care and respect for yourself and turn your new, heightened energy into a powerful force for achieving all your desired intentions.

Getting creative with your Power Foods may take some time. This is to be expected. Getting into the kitchen is your first step. Trying a recipe once, twice or three times before it works out the way you hoped it would is also part of this process. Never get discouraged, for persistence will lead you to some magical results. Most of my recipes came from years of experimenting. Countless recipes were recreated, redesigned and recalibrated to fit my Power of Food philosophy that recipes should be both easy to create and taste great. The recipes in this book will help guide you every step of the way in your creative process and have you excited to share your many creations.

ACTION STEP 10.
TURN UP THE LOVE

Over the years my feelings toward food preparation grew from being a hate relationship to an abundant love relationship. Now every moment I am in my kitchen making tasty creations for my family and friends, I feel like I am climbing the highest mountain and yelling from the summit for all to hear. That might sound a bit over-the-top, but it is the truth. My kitchen gives me great joy, and I feel very powerful when playing with Power Foods in ways I know will nourish my mind and body. It's time to get into your kitchen and feel the love.

1. Pick one recipe from *The Power of Food* recipe section and make a grocery list.
2. Go out and buy the ingredients on your list. Buy double the amount so you have extra ingredients on hand for the next time.
3. Get in your kitchen and start creating.
4. Share your creation with as many people as possible. It is through sharing that I grew to love being creative in the kitchen.
5. Repeat steps 1 to 4 two more times this week.

WHAT YOU CAN EXPECT: The more time you spend in your kitchen creating delicious treats with your Power Foods, the more you will feel energized and excited to keep experimenting. You will also find yourself moving up the Power of Food 80/20 rule scale with ease, from 51% to 80%.

DAILY FOOD JOURNAL

TODAY I ATE	LIVING FOOD ✔	PROCESSED FOOD X
Cereal and dairy milk		X X
Power Food mix (added to cereal)	✔	
Sandwich (bread, ham, cheese, lettuce, tomato, hemp seeds)	✔ ✔ ✔	X X X
Muffin with glass of hemp milk	✔	X
Handful of almonds	✔	
Grilled chicken with steamed broccoli and red pepper	✔ ✔	X
	Total ✔ 8	Total X 7
My daily total	51%	

If you have more ✔ than **X** you are above 51%. What was your % for the day?

5. TRACK YOUR SUCCESS DAILY

The last step to reaching the Magic Number is tracking your daily success. Here is an example of a page from a Power of Food Daily Food Journal (see 202 for a form you use yourself). This journal makes it easy for you to track your daily success for living each day at 51%.

Each day, list everything you eat. Then place an X or a checkmark beside each food, depending on whether the food is living or processed. For example, if you ate a bowl of cereal or oatmeal, you would put an X beside this in the Processed Food column. (Yes, is oatmeal is a processed food unless it is steel-cut or stone-ground.) If you added 1 Tbsp (15 mL) of your Power Foods mix to your cereal, you would add this to your journal and place a checkmark beside it in the Living Food column. If you had a ham and cheese sandwich with lettuce, tomatoes and 1 tbsp (15 mL) hemp seeds, you'd put three Xs in the Processed

Food column (for the bread, ham and cheese) and three checkmarks in the Living Food column (for the lettuce, tomatoes and hemp seeds).

At the end of the day, count the number of Xs and checkmarks and record the total at the bottom of the journal. If you have more checkmarks than Xs, you've reached the Magic Number of 51% or higher.

Do you see how quickly you can start to reach the Magic Number of 51% and much higher right away? It is all about what you add to your diet, not about changing what you enjoy eating that is an X. You still get to eat your ham and cheese sandwich, but adding more nutrient-rich Power Foods helps you reach 51%. I predict that your Xs will eventually start to disappear, leaving you with only checkmarks!

ACTION STEP 11.

TRACK YOUR PROGRESS

I began using food journals back in my days of endless dieting. They were usually meant for counting calories and always left me more confused. I started using my Power of Food *Daily Food Journal* while in Golden. It allowed me to gain a deeper love and respect for the foods I was choosing to eat and made me want to learn more about the power of food. Here's how to start your own *Daily Food Journal*.

1. If you haven't already, read the sample entries in the Power of Food *Daily Food Journal* on page 41.
2. Visit PowerofFood.com and print out your free single-page sample copy of the *Daily Food Journal*.
3. Make enough copies of the page to last 30 days.
4. Begin recording your daily food consumption of living versus processed foods and see how you do each day, reaching for the Magic Number of 51%.
5. At the end of each week, add up your totals from each day and see how your week's results look. Have you reached or passed 51% for the entire week?
6. At the end of 30 days, add up your totals for the entire month and see how you progressed through the weeks.
7. Print out another month's worth of journal pages and keep going toward your 80/20 goal.

WHAT YOU CAN EXPECT: By tracking your daily intake of Power Foods, you will begin to grow a stronger relationship to healthier eating and see more clearly where your diet can be improved. Your feelings of success will build momentum as you begin living with a renewed excitement and energy around your healthy results.

The Power of Food *Daily Food Journal* is not a calorie counting system, and it is not designed to keep track of portion sizes. Your only goal is to increase the number of times you eat Power Foods on a daily basis. This will allow you to begin controlling your blood sugar and enable your body and mind to begin receiving the nutrients it has been starving for. Using this journal daily will allow you to remove your countless food cravings and enjoy some freedom from your unhealthy food addictions.

BRINGING IT ALL TOGETHER

Once you have gone through the five steps to achieving the Magic Number of 51%, you will have strengthened your relationship with your own health and built up enough momentum to begin living closer to 80% living food or beyond. To recap, here are those five steps one more time:

1. Discover four to six key Power Foods within the six Power of Food Groups.
2. Eat your four to six Power Foods as a healthy snack throughout your day.
3. Begin to add each of the four to six Power Foods into the foods you eat.
4. Get creative with your Power Foods by trying some Power of Food recipes.
5. Use the Power of Food *Daily Food Journal* to track your success.

The 80/20 rule is meant to help guide you to achieving the success you desire right away. Reaching the Magic Number of 51% is attainable right now, and your ability to feel more energized, stronger, fitter and happier is only days away. Now it is time to take action and check out all the goodies that await you in the more than 100 Power of Food recipes. See you on the other side!

There are only two ways to live your life. One is as though nothing is a miracle. The other is as though everything is a miracle. —**Albert Einstein**

THE POWER

OF FOOD

RECIPES

THINKING OF MYSELF AS A CHEF is a bit strange, but I do. Once upon a time my kitchen repertoire consisted of preparing macaroni and cheese, making peanut butter and jam sandwiches or pouring milk over cereal. To go from that place to discovering how to use living food in creative ways has been extremely empowering.

Learning to be skilled in the kitchen did not happen overnight. In my first few years of learning how to cook, I found myself preparing a lot of stir-fries, soups and stews. As I became more active in the mountains and continued to add healthy Power Foods to my diet, I slowly moved away from always heating and cooking my food. Instead I began to prepare many of my meals by trying to retain the full amount of nutrients available to maximize my ability to stay strong, fit, trim and energized. This led me to experiment with all types of Power Foods found within the six Power of Food Groups. Hemp seeds, ginger, goji berries, beets, kale, almonds and chia seeds are just a few of the high-energy foods that began to appear regularly in my daily diet. I was starting to wake up each and every morning feeling abundantly happy and healthy, and I knew the foods I was eating were playing a very large role.

FOOD WITHOUT LABELS

In the pages that follow I share with you over 100 of my favourite Power of Food recipes. A select few of these recipes are from the days when I first started cooking, such as my Lentil Shepherd's Pie (page 124) and Split Pea Soup (page 134). The more recent creations Goji Chia Jerky (page 95) and Barbecue Kale Ribs (page 168) are two perfect examples of how far I have taken experimenting with Power Foods in my kitchen.

Yes, most of these recipes are vegan, vegetarian and raw, but I am not a fan of putting labels on them. Our mind has a funny way of sabotaging our thoughts. Let's test out this theory. When I say vegan, what comes to your mind? How about raw? I know how I used to think. *That's crazy, those people are way too fanatical. Eating like a rabbit is not for me,* and so on. My mind held me back for years from getting healthier and not only when it came to food. This self-sabotage happened with regard to fitness, at work and in relationships with family and friends.

To avoid the saboteur in most of us, I prefer to present my favourite Power of Food recipes with no labels. All you need to know is that these recipes allowed me to reach a new level of health and happiness and are now doing

the same for thousands of others. I am mindful of the need for recipes to be fun and creative, but what was most important for my progression in the kitchen was the ease with which a recipe could be prepared. So their simplicity is what you will notice about the 100-plus creations in the pages that follow.

You will also notice that several of my recipes use five ingredients or less and take less than five minutes to prepare—for instance, magical goodies such as my Raw-Raw Brownies (page 159) and Mooove Over Mooo Milk (page 56). Keep an eye out for the 5 in 5 symbol (5 in 5) to find the 5 in 5 recipes. Another key attribute of these Power of Food recipes is that they call for easy-to-find ingredients. After all, what good is a recipe if it uses several ingredients you have never heard of or have no idea where to find? All of my recipes are easy to prepare, using ingredients that are familiar and easy to find. If there is an ingredient you don't know about, google it and

discover something new. Then on your next visit to the grocery store, ask an employee where you can find it and give it a try. Each ingredient in the Power of Food recipes is there for a reason—it is powerful.

These recipes will help guide you away from a diet of processed foods and toward healthier living foods. If you are already eating a diet rich in living foods, many of these recipes will help you become more creative using living foods and get you excited to try some new tricks. Once you have a good handle on what living foods are, how to use them daily and how to use them creatively, you will be sure to experience a new level of supercharged energy that will last a lifetime.

ABOUT THE RECIPES

The recipes are divided into six sections based on the six Power of Food Groups: nuts, seeds, grains, legumes, fruits and vegetables. I offer unique creations to choose from in each food group, making it easy for you to find the foods you are looking for and incorporate them into your daily diet.

Many years ago in working with clients I would overload them with too many ingredients. I would show up at their door for an in-home Power of Food session with two big bins of all the key Power Foods I was eating, including 15 different grains, 12 different legumes, 15 different vegetables, a dozen fruits and 10 different nuts and seeds. Since then I have learned to keep things simple. The easier a recipe or system is, the more likely you are to give it a try. Here, along with the recipes, I share with you my top four Power Foods from each of the six Power of Food Groups. For example, when you flip through the recipe section on seeds, you will notice special sidebars highlighting the power of hemp seeds, flaxseeds, chia seeds and sesame seeds. Each sidebar explores what makes this food powerful, why you should care and how to use it. It also offers suggestions for daily use and guidelines for keeping the food fresh.

Another great feature you can look forward to is how I have grouped many of the Power of Food recipes to follow each of the key Power Foods highlighted. For example, near the sidebar on the power of hemp seeds, you will find some of my favourite hemp seed recipes. This allows you to get started right away with a given Power Food you are interested in.

KITCHEN EQUIPMENT

One of the main reasons people do not enjoy experimenting with food is because their kitchens are overcrowded with too many gadgets and provide very little space in which to work. From my own experience and from speaking with hundreds of clients over the years, I have found that once you begin to reduce the clutter and remove unnecessary items from your kitchen, preparing healthy meals becomes a little less daunting and more manageable. The recipes you are about to discover use primarily four kitchen gadgets, which you can use to whip up hundreds of simple and tasty meals without any of the clutter frustration. In no particular order, those gadgets are:

- **Food Processor.** Ideally your food processor will be large enough to hold 12 to 14 cups (3 to 3.5 L). Many of my recipes can be used to prepare meals in bulk, to ensure you have leftovers to enjoy the following day or enough to feed a large family. When looking to purchase a food processor, think about quality over price. I have gone through about a dozen low-quality food processors over the years. They cost about $50, but you end up spending more in the end by needing to replace them after only a few months. Purchasing a good-quality food processor with a strong motor, such as a Cuisinart or the Breville Sous Chef, will save you money in the long run and make creating healthy treats and meals a breeze.

- **Blender.** In my kitchen the blender is king. I use it two or three times a day preparing many of the recipes you are about to discover. Just as with a food processor, quality is crucial. Ideally your blender should be strong enough to break down cell walls of food, such as the Vitamix, Blendtec or NutriBullet brands. This ensures that the foods are easier to digest and provide you with more sustained energy.

- **Coffee Grinder.** Get yourself a coffee grinder to use specifically for grinding nuts, herbs and seeds. If you use one that regularly grinds coffee, this will alter the

THE POWER OF FOOD

flavours in your recipes. Do some research and find yourself a nice large coffee grinder with a deep lid. The deeper the lid, the more it can hold. I always have 1 to 2 cups (250 to 500 mL) of ground flaxseeds, ground sesame seeds or ground chia seeds and a few ground nuts on hand ready to add into my favourite meals.

- **Dehydrator.** If the blender is king, my dehydrator is the queen. Twenty-four hours a day my dehydrator is working away, pulling moisture from and preserving many of my cookies, crackers, sprouted nuts and countless other Power of Food treats. Removing the moisture from food enables you to create different textures and countless possibilities while ensuring the foods will last several weeks or months to be enjoyed as needed. As with all kitchen equipment, quality is crucial as well as size. Look for a dehydrator that has enough space to hold multiple creations at once, preferably in a square housing. The dehydrator should also provide even heating from front to back, top to bottom. Stay away from poor-quality dehydrators to avoid uneven heating. I've used my nine-tray Excalibur dehydrator for years and it continues to hold up as my favourite model on the market.

A notable mention must go to the juicer, another kitchen gadget that in time, if you do not use one already, will become a part of your daily routine. A juicer is not necessary for the recipes in this book. However, juicing is a very big act of love, and using a slow juicer as opposed to a high-friction speed juicer will ensure you maximize your daily intake of nutrients.

To introduce or upgrade one or more of these kitchen gadgets may be a financial investment for you and your family. If this is the case, I suggest you look at a few of the recipes you would like to try and make your equipment upgrades one item at a time to fit your budget. By getting into your kitchen and using just one of these Power of Food gadgets, you will gain motivation and find yourself on the way to better health.

As for the cost of groceries, I often get asked whether eating healthy is expensive. When I first wanted to get healthier, I automatically had the mindset that it must be more expensive to eat healthy. I have since discovered this is not the case. Here's my short response to this question: once I started eating living foods, I began eating less. Due to the fact that they supply more high-quality vital nutrients in ways that are easier to digest, living foods help reduce your sugar and other food cravings and leave you feeling satisfied without needing to overeat. The result is less need to buy large amounts of processed foods to try to stay energized, a reduced grocery bill and cupboards full of living nutrients to nourish your body and mind.

All there is left to do now is turn the pages and start exploring. Just be warned: your mouth is about to start salivating!

BEETS BLACK GINGER ALMONDS

BEANS amaranth

vegetables

chickpeas BLUEBERRIES GARLIC AVOCADOS PISTACHIOS BROWN

seeds fruits RICE

GOJI PECANS GREEN PEAS

nuts

BERRIES grains

WHOLE OATS KALE CASHEWS

QUINOA LENTILS

COCONUT

legumes

THE POWER OF PISTACHIOS

WHY YOU SHOULD CARE Has your hair started falling out? This is a question for both the guys and girls out there. Mine did when I was 24 years old. If only I had known about essential fatty acids (EFAs) back when I was in my twenties. Not all of us are meant to keep our hair, but if you want a fighting chance, consuming a healthy dose of good-quality EFAs from pistachios will help. If you want healthy-looking hair and the ability to keep it on your head a little longer, pistachios just may become your new best friend.

HOW TO USE Pistachios are great as a snack. You can also chop or grind pistachios to create any number of creative and delicious recipes. I often shell my fresh pistachios ahead of time so they are ready when I want to add them to a recipe. You can even buy them already shelled.

Breakfast: Add some chopped pistachios into your pancake mix or into your next batch of muffins or cookies. Or sprinkle some into your morning smoothie or cereal.

Lunch/Snack: Eat them raw. Add chopped pistachios into your soup or salad. Sprinkle some ground pistachios on top of your sandwich. Add them to whatever you like to eat and feel a healthy boost in energy without restricting your diet.

Dinner: Tonight when you sit down for dinner, add ¼ cup (60 mL) of chopped pistachios to your salad or stir-fry, and see how this enhances the flavour while giving you a nutritional boost with every bite.

HOW TO STORE Due to the high content of EFAs in pistachios, it is important to store them in the refrigerator or freezer. They will keep in the refrigerator for up to 3 months and in the freezer for up to 6 months.

Green-tinged pistachios, with their odd half-open shells, are a versatile and tasty nut. Not only do they provide a healthy dose of essential fatty acids, they also contain an ideal supply of iron and are known to help lower cholesterol when eaten fresh, before being roasted or salted. Fun to shell, pistachios are also a great source of protein and fibre. Being loaded with vital nutrients, pistachios make a great addition to your diet.

PISTACHIO MANGO SALSA

MAKES 4 CUPS (1 L)

PLACE ALL THE INGREDIENTS into a medium bowl and gently mix together. Be careful not to mash up the avocado too much. That's it—your salsa is ready to serve. Enjoy with Hemptastic Crackers (page 79).

power food tip *Try adding any number of seeds or nuts to the mix to create salsas for every occasion.*

1 mango, peeled, pitted and diced

1 avocado, peeled, pitted and diced

2 medium tomatoes, diced

½ red onion, diced

2 cloves garlic, minced

½ cup (125 mL) cilantro, chopped

½ cup (125 mL) pistachios, chopped

1 tbsp (15 mL) lemon juice

½ tsp (2 mL) Himalayan crystal salt

CREAMY PISTACHIO POTATO SALAD

MAKES 4 CUPS (1 L)

MAKE SURE TO CUT the potatoes into small bite-size pieces. Steam the potatoes until they are slightly tender, about 5 minutes. You do not want the potatoes too mushy for this recipe. Refrigerate the potatoes for 20 minutes to let cool. Blend the remaining ingredients in a blender or food processor. After the potatoes have cooled, place the potatoes and the blended dressing into a large mixing bowl and gently mix together. Serve this tasty salad with my Macho Man Loaf (page 103). Store any leftovers in an airtight glass container in the refrigerator for up to 4 days.

～～～

power food tip Add ¼ cup (60 mL) seeds or nuts to boost the flavour and nutritional value of every bite.

2 cups (500 mL) red potatoes, chopped

¼ cup (60 mL) pistachios, chopped

3 tbsp (45 mL) dill, chopped

1 tbsp (15 mL) parsley, chopped

2 tbsp (30 mL) lemon juice

2 tbsp (30 mL) lemon zest

¼ cup (60 mL) tahini

2 tbsp (30 mL) prepared mustard

½ tsp (2 mL) Himalayan crystal salt

THE POWER OF ALMONDS

WHY YOU SHOULD CARE Recently a client asked me what I eat when travelling. I take a number of foods with me, but none is more important than almonds. The number one thing many of us do when we are stressed is eat, and being on the road can be stressful. Almonds are my go-to stress snack when I am sitting stuck in traffic or rushing to make an appointment. A handful of almonds satisfies my stress response and helps relax me into a calmer state. Try eating a handful of almonds the next time you're looking for something when feeling stressed.

HOW TO USE I prefer to consume my almonds after they have been soaked for 12 to 24 hours to remove unwanted moulds and to increase their digestibility. I soak them overnight and then place them into the dehydrator to restore their crunchiness and remove any moisture. You can use your oven set at the lowest temperature for the same purpose. If you don't want to go through the hassle of soaking your almonds, don't. They are still much healthier than a bag of chips.

Breakfast: Try a piece of sprouted grain bread spread with almond butter. How about using almond milk in your smoothie or over cereal for tomorrow's breakfast? When in doubt, add a handful to your cereal or oatmeal to power up your morning.

Lunch/Snack: Add shredded or whole almonds to your salad or bowl of soup. Spreading a little almond butter on a sandwich is a nice way to enjoy some extra energy. Next time you make a morning almond milk smoothie, make a little extra to enjoy for your lunch or a powerful snack.

Dinner: Soak 1 cup (250 mL) almonds overnight and turn them into a pâté or tasty spread to go with your dinner. After the almonds have soaked for 12 hours, discard the water and blend the almonds in a food processor until smooth. Not only does this turn almonds into instant almond butter, by adding herbs or honey you can go either savoury or sweet to meet your breakfast, lunch, snacking or dinner needs.

HOW TO STORE Store almonds in the refrigerator for up to 3 months or the freezer for up to 6 months to preserve their essential fatty acids. Keep a small jar in the door of the refrigerator for quick daily access, right next to the hemp seeds and ground flaxseeds.

High in protein, almonds are a great recovery food for your muscles and give you lasting energy through their high iron content. Golden brown and symmetrical, they are also a great source of calcium, vitamin E and essential fatty acids. Almonds are sweet and make great milk or butter that even children love.

MOOOVE OVER MOOO MILK

MAKES 2 CUPS (500 ML)

IN 2 SEPARATE BOWLS, soak the almonds in 2 cups (500 mL) water and the dates in 1½ cups (375 mL) water overnight. The next morning, drain and rinse the almonds. Place all the ingredients, including the water the dates soaked in, into a blender. Blend until smooth, adding more water as needed until the mixture reaches your desired consistency. Place the liquid into a large cheesecloth or nut bag and, using your hands, squeeze out the almond milk over a large bowl. After you have squeezed out as much milk as possible, place the milk into a glass container and store it in the refrigerator. Almond milk will keep for 3 to 4 days in the refrigerator.

1 cup (250 mL) almonds
¼ cup (60 mL) pitted dates, chopped
1 tsp (5 mL) honey
½ tsp (2 mL) pure vanilla extract

Pictured on facing page.

power food tip *The leftover pulp may be stored in the freezer and used to make any number of delicious baked goods, among them Zucchini Nut Muffins (page 60).*

MOJO POWER SNACK PACK

MAKES 4 CUPS (1 L) OF GOODNESS

PLACE ALL THE INGREDIENTS into a large mixing bowl and mix together. Place the mixture into a large freezer bag and store in the refrigerator for daily use. Portion out a daily serving and use as a powerful energy snack. I tend to eat about 2 cups (500 mL) daily, spread throughout my day.

1 cup (250 mL) almonds, whole
1 cup (250 mL) walnuts, whole
1 cup (250 mL) dried goji berries
    or cranberries
½ cup (125 mL) cacao nibs

ONLINE BONUS

Visit PowerofFood.com to watch a video on how to prepare this recipe.

power food tip *Try making double the amount and leaving some at the office to be sure to avoid any mid-afternoon energy crashes.*

MUSHROOM ALMOND STUFFING

MAKES 4 CUPS (1 L)

IN A SMALL BOWL, mix the olive oil, soy sauce and vinegar to make a marinade for the mushrooms. Add the mushrooms and refrigerate overnight. The next day, discard the marinade and blend the marinated mushrooms in a food processor with the almonds and fresh herbs. Add the carrots and celery to the food processor and mix. Add more olive oil or some flax oil to the mixture until it reaches your desired consistency. Stored in an airtight glass container in the refrigerator, this stuffing will keep for 2 to 3 days.

~~~~~~~~

power food tip *Add some raisins or dried cranberries to your stuffing to give it a little sweetness. This stuffing goes great with baked butternut squash or spinach salad (as a topping).*

¼ cup (60 mL) extra virgin olive oil

¼ cup (60 mL) soy sauce

1 tbsp (15 mL) apple cider vinegar

2 portobello mushrooms, chopped

3 cups (750 mL) almonds, chopped

2 tsp (10 mL) oregano, chopped

2 tsp (10 mL) rosemary, chopped

2 tsp (10 mL) parsley, chopped

½ cup (125 mL) carrots, chopped

½ cup (125 mL) celery, chopped

ALMOND AND HEMP SPREAD

MAKES 2 CUPS (500 mL)

SOAK THE ALMONDS in 2 cups (500 mL) water for 24 hours. After they have soaked, drain and rinse the almonds, discarding the water. Place all the ingredients except the hemp seeds into a food processor. Blend to a smooth paste and then add the hemp seeds. Continue to blend, adding more water as needed until the mixture reaches your desired consistency. Stored in an airtight glass container in the refrigerator, your spread will keep for 3 to 4 days.

~~~~~~~~

power food tip *This spread is fantastic as a high-energy mid-afternoon snack or lunch option. Add a healthy scoop to your wraps or sandwiches or over my Super Veggie Quinoa Crackers (page 171).*

1 cup (250 mL) almonds

2 tbsp (30 mL) almond butter

2 tsp (10 mL) grated ginger

Juice of ½ lemon

½ cup (125 mL) water

¼ cup (60 mL) flax oil, hemp oil or
extra virgin olive oil

½ tsp (2 mL) Himalayan crystal salt

½ cup (125 mL) hemp seeds

Pictured on facing page.

ZUCCHINI NUT MUFFINS

MAKES 12 MUFFINS

SOAK THE CHOPPED DATES in ½ cup (125 mL) water for 30 minutes and then purée both in a blender. Preheat the oven to 350°F (180°C). Place paper liners in a 12-cup muffin pan. In a medium bowl, combine all the dry ingredients. In a separate bowl, combine all the wet ingredients. Mix each bowl well. Add the wet ingredients to the dry ingredients and mix together. Spoon the batter into the prepared muffin pan and bake in the preheated oven for 30 minutes. Let cool and serve. Place your muffins in an airtight glass container and store in the refrigerator for quick access. Feel free to store 6 muffins in the freezer to be eaten at a later date as a quick on-the-go snack.

power food tip *Replace the muffin pan with an 8-inch (20 cm) square baking dish coated with coconut oil to create a yummy cake variation. Alternatively, ladle this batter into a large frying pan with some coconut oil to make delicious pancakes.*

½ cup (125 mL) pitted dates, chopped

1½ cups (375 mL) brown rice flour

1 cup (250 mL) almond pulp
  (see page 56)

¼ cup (60 mL) coconut sugar

2 tbsp (30 mL) hemp seeds

2 tsp (10 mL) baking powder

½ tsp (2 mL) baking soda

¼ cup (60 mL) raisins

½ cup (125 mL) mixed nuts
  (pecans, walnuts, almonds), chopped

1 cup (250 mL) hemp milk (page 81)

2 eggs

½ cup (125 mL) zucchini, shredded

¼ tsp (1 mL) pure vanilla extract

HIGH-ENERGY TRAIL MIX

MAKES 3 CUPS (750 ML)

PLACE ALL THE INGREDIENTS into an airtight glass container and mix. Store in the refrigerator between snacking sessions to preserve the freshness of this mix as long as possible. Now all you need to do is grab a handful to help control your blood sugar when you get your next food craving.

power food tip *Get creative. Add any number of dried fruits, nuts and seeds to the mix to create different variations. I take a bag of my trail mix on the road with me everywhere I go.*

½ cup (125 mL) almonds

½ cup (125 mL) walnuts

½ cup (125 mL) sunflower seeds

½ cup (125 mL) pumpkin seeds

½ cup (125 mL) dried cranberries

½ cup (125 mL) cacao nibs

Pictured on facing page.

THE POWER OF PECANS

WHY YOU SHOULD CARE Do you find the meals you create becoming a little boring? Are you eating the same things over and over again? Getting bored of the food you eat is the first sign you will soon be spending too much money at restaurants or for takeout. Pecans are my go-to food when I want to get more creative with many of my recipes. They add a lot of flavour and can be ground into a flour to be used as a thickener for soups, sauces and gravies. I make veggie burgers with them and even an ever-so-tasty pizza crust. The next time you pick up the phone to order in a pizza or grab your jacket to go eat out, think of how you can use pecans to liven up one of your old-time recipes.

HOW TO USE Just like almonds, pecans make a great snack. You can consume them in their whole state (shelled, of course) or as a butter or milk. Each option will provide you with a host of healthy benefits that should not be missed. Tomorrow when you wake up, add 2 cups (500 mL) water and ½ cup (125 mL) pecans to a blender and see how it tastes when blended together. Too good!

Breakfast: I love sprinkling roasted pecans over my pancakes or adding them to my homemade breads. Here is another Power of Food trick for you: in a coffee grinder (preferably not used for coffee, for taste purposes), grind ¼ cup (60 mL) pecans into flour and place the flour into your morning cereal. Now add water instead of milk to enjoy an instant maple-like pecan milk that is extremely delicious.

Lunch/Snack: A pecan smoothie is a great idea for snacking on throughout the day. It will sustain your energy so you avoid any low points. I often enhance the taste of my salads with some freshly ground pecans as the garnish. I'll even load the top of the salad with a big scoop of pecan butter for a powerful energy kick. Use the same method as for almond pâté or spread (page 55).

Dinner: Add chopped pecans to any recipe and taste a powerful boost of flavour.

HOW TO STORE To preserve the essential fatty acids contained in pecans, store them in the refrigerator for up to 3 months or in the freezer for up to 6 months. Keep some in the door of the refrigerator for quick access, preferably next to your almonds, hemp seeds and ground flaxseeds.

Pecans, rich-brown in colour when shelled, are also rich in a number of essential nutrients. With an abundant amount of fibre in every bite, this nut is a must for increasing your energy levels throughout the day. With their natural maple flavour, pecans are a versatile addition to many recipes.

PECAN CHOCOLATE SPICE COOKIES

MAKES 8 COOKIES

SOAK THE PECANS in 3 cups (750 mL) of water for 1 hour. After they have soaked, drain and rinse the pecans, discarding the water. Blend the soaked pecans with the remaining ingredients in a food processor until the mixture becomes slightly sticky. Place large, individual spoonfuls of cookie batter on a cutting board. Press down into your desired shape and serve. That's it—no baking required. Stored in an airtight glass container in the refrigerator, these cookies will keep for 4 to 6 days. If stored in the freezer, they will keep for several months.

power food tip *Try replacing the pecans with almonds to change up the recipe.*

1½ cups (375 mL) pecans

1 cup (250 mL) pitted dates, chopped

¼ cup (60 mL) hemp seeds

½ cup (125 mL) shredded coconut

½ tsp (2 mL) grated ginger

½ tsp (2 mL) pure vanilla extract

2 tbsp (30 mL) cacao powder

1 tsp (5 mL) cinnamon

½ tsp (2 mL) nutmeg

½ tsp (2 mL) Himalayan crystal salt

2 tbsp (30 mL) water

SWEET ROASTED PECANS

MAKES 2 CUPS (500 ML)

PREHEAT THE OVEN to 250°F (120°C). Spread the pecans evenly onto a large baking sheet and place on the oven's centre rack. Mix the pecans occasionally until they begin to brown, about 5 minutes. Once they are browned, place the pecans into a large mixing bowl with the coconut oil, sugar and salt. Mix all the ingredients until each pecan has been coated. Return the pecans to the baking sheet and roast in the oven for an additional 2 minutes. Set the pecans aside to cool for 10 minutes. Once cooled, store in an airtight glass container in the refrigerator. These roasted pecans will keep for up to 1 month.

~~~~~

power food tip   *You can use this recipe as a snack, or try the roasted pecans as a topping or garnish for other Power of Food recipes. You can even add some hemp seeds to the mix before the final 2 minutes of baking.*

2 cups (500 mL) pecan halves

2 tbsp (30 mL) coconut oil

2 tbsp (30 mL) raw cane sugar

¼ tsp (1 mL) Himalayan crystal salt

THE POWER OF CASHEWS

WHY YOU SHOULD CARE I grew up drinking 2% milk, because that's what everyone did in my family. Now I mainly drink nut and seed milks—because they make me feel fantastic. Cashews are a great addition to a blender full of water to create a delicious after-school or morning energy drink. Next time your child comes running through the door looking for something nutritious to drink, give them the heart-healthy benefits of cashews, blended with water and a banana. Just wait to see how they enjoy it!

HOW TO USE Like almonds and pecans, cashews are also a great energy snack eaten whole. If you are eating them whole as a snack, avoid salted or sweetened cashews. Besides whole, cashews are also available in pieces, as butter, as milk or as oil. Each option will provide you with a host of healthy benefits that should not be missed. I use cashews in Power of Food recipes to create smooth, creamy textures without needing to use dairy.

Breakfast: Enjoy a morning boost from cashew milk. You can also add whole, chopped or ground cashews to your morning oatmeal to set you up for an energetic day.

Lunch/Snack: Add sliced cashews to your salad or eat them whole as a snack. A small handful is all it takes to satisfy the biggest of hungers. Spread a little cashew butter on your next midday sandwich or mix a dollop into a bowl of soup to make it a little creamier.

Dinner: Add chopped cashews to your stir-fry, rice bowl or pasta sauce, and look forward to achieving more energy with ease.

HOW TO STORE To preserve the essential fatty acids found in cashews, store them in the refrigerator for up to 3 months or in the freezer for up to 6 months.

Cashews are a well-rounded nut in that they offer you a balanced supply of essential fatty acids, fibre and quality protein. These smooth, kidney-shaped nuts are also a good source of copper and iron. Plus cashews are full of flavour.

IN-THE-RAW RANCH DIP

MAKES 1 CUP (250 ML)

PLACE ALL THE INGREDIENTS into a blender and blend. Add water as needed until the mixture reaches your desired consistency. Store this dip in an airtight glass container in the refrigerator and consume within 3 days.

~~~~

power food tip *Use this dip as a delicious dressing for any of the Power of Food salad recipes or to add protein and punch to a wrap or sandwich.*

1 cup (250 mL) cashews

¼ cup (60 mL) extra virgin olive oil

¼ cup (60 mL) parsley, chopped

¼ cup (60 mL) dill, chopped

1 clove garlic, minced

1 tbsp (15 mL) lemon juice

1 tbsp (15 mL) flax oil

½ tsp (2 mL) Himalayan crystal salt

MORNING BOOSTER SMOOTHIE

MAKES 2 CUPS (500 mL)

PLACE ALL THE INGREDIENTS into a blender and blend. Add more water as needed until the mixture reaches your desired consistency. Store your smoothie in an airtight glass jar in the refrigerator and consume within 24 hours.

〜〜〜

power food tip *Try making double the amount and having the second portion later in the day for lunch or a snack. Add in 1 tbsp (15 mL) cacao powder to make this into a chocolate version.*

½ cup (125 mL) spinach, chopped

½ cup (125 mL) blueberries

1 tbsp (15 mL) flax oil

3 tbsp (45 mL) cashews, ground

2 tbsp (30 mL) hemp seeds

2 cups (500 mL) water

Pictured on facing page.

ONLINE BONUS

Visit PowerofFood.com to watch a video on how to prepare this recipe.

MAKE-IT-YOURSELF MAYO

MAKES 1 CUP (250 mL)

SOAK THE CASHEWS in 2 cups (500 mL) water for 1 hour. After they have soaked, drain and rinse the cashews, discarding the water. Place all the ingredients into a food processor and blend. Add more water as needed until the mixture reaches your desired consistency. Store this mayo in an airtight glass container in the refrigerator and consume within 3 days.

〜〜〜

power food tip *Try this mayo as a vegetable dip or on top of my Ultimate Veggie Burgers (page 73).*

1 cup (250 mL) cashews

1 tbsp (15 mL) lemon juice

¼ cup (60 mL) flax oil, hemp oil or
     extra virgin olive oil

1 clove garlic, minced

1 tbsp (15 mL) prepared mustard

¼ cup (60 mL) water

ULTIMATE CHOCOLATE MOUSSE

MAKES 2 CUPS (500 ML)

SOAK THE CASHEWS in 2 cups (500 mL) water for 1 hour. After they have soaked, drain and rinse the cashews, discarding the water. Place the soaked cashews and the remaining ingredients in a food processor and blend. Add more water as needed until the mixture reaches your desired consistency. Store your mousse in an airtight glass container in the refrigerator and consume within 3 days.

1 cup (250 mL) cashews

¼ cup (60 mL) cacao powder

1 tbsp (15 mL) honey

½ tsp (2 mL) pure vanilla extract

½ cup (125 mL) + 1 tbsp (15 mL) water

Pictured on facing page.

power food tip *Serve with fresh seasonal berries such as blueberries. You can also add, as a topping, 1 tbsp (15 mL) hemp seeds or ground almonds per serving to boost the flavour and nutritional value of cashews.*

STRAWBERRY CASHEW CREAM

MAKES 2½ CUPS (625 ML)

SOAK THE CASHEWS in 2 cups (500 mL) water for 1 hour. After they have soaked, drain and rinse the cashews, discarding the water. Place the soaked cashews and the remaining ingredients into a food processor and blend. Add more water as needed until the mixture reaches your desired consistency. Store your cream in an airtight glass container in the refrigerator and consume within 3 days.

2 cups (500 mL) cashews

1 cup (250 mL) strawberries

½ cup (125 mL) water

1 tsp (5 mL) pure vanilla extract

power food tip *This cream tastes great inside the Active Kids Banana Crêpes (page 154) or overtop some fresh melon.*

AMAZING STRAWBERRY CHEESECAKE

MAKES ONE 10-INCH (25 CM) ROUND CAKE

CRUST Soak the dates in 4 cups (1 L) water for 1 hour, reserving the water for both the date paste and the topping. Grind the almonds in a coffee grinder (not used for coffee). Place the soaked dates into a food processor with the cacao powder and blend together. Add a little of the reserved date water to the blender to create a paste, but don't make the mixture too moist. Place the date paste in a mixing bowl and mix in the ground almonds until a batter is formed. Evenly spread the batter into a 10-inch (25 cm) pie dish.

TOPPING Soak the cashews in 4 cups (1 L) water for 1 hour. After they have soaked, drain and rinse the cashews, discarding the water. Place the soaked cashews into a blender and blend. Add ¼ cup (60 mL) of the reserved date water, the maple syrup, the strawberries and the salt. Blend until smooth. Add more date water until the mixture reaches a smooth texture but is not too runny. Place the mixture overtop of the pie crust, and top with the extra strawberries and almonds. Refrigerate for 2 hours and serve.

~~~~~~~~~

power food tip You can make any variety of cheesecake just by changing the fruit you add, such as banana, apple, peach or blueberry. It's your choice. You can even change the crust by replacing the almonds with pecans or another favourite nut or seed.

CRUST

2 cups (500 mL) pitted dates, chopped

1 cup (250 mL) almonds

2 tbsp (30 mL) cacao powder

TOPPING

2 cups (500 mL) cashews

2 tbsp (30 mL) maple syrup

1 cup (250 mL) strawberries

½ tsp (2 mL) Himalayan crystal salt

Extra strawberries and almonds
  for garnish

ULTIMATE VEGGIE BURGERS

MAKES 8 PATTIES

PLACE ALL THE INGREDIENTS into a food processor and blend together. If the mixture is too wet, add more quinoa or walnuts as needed to absorb the extra moisture. Next place the mixture into a mixing bowl and, using your hands, create 8 burger-size patties. Place your patties in the dehydrator for 24 hours. If using an oven, place them on a baking sheet (no foil needed) and bake at the lowest temperature for 45 minutes. If the burgers are still moist after baking, flip them and bake for another 30 minutes, or until they are done.

2 cups (500 mL) walnuts

2 cups (500 mL) quinoa, cooked

3 medium tomatoes, diced

1 medium onion, diced

2 cloves garlic, minced

¼ cup (60 mL) parsley, chopped

2 tbsp (30 mL) cumin

~~~~~~~~

power food tip   *Instead of using processed buns for these burger patties, try using pieces of Swiss chard. It tastes great and is a very healthy alternative.*

WALNUT CHOCOLATE TRUFFLES

MAKES 6 TRUFFLES

PLACE ALL THE INGREDIENTS except the coating into a food processor and blend together. Using your hands, roll the mixture into small balls half the size of a golf ball and set aside. On a large plate, place your choice of the following: ground almonds or hemp seeds, shredded coconut or cacao powder. Roll each truffle around the plate until coated. Store in an airtight container in the refrigerator. Eat your truffles within 4 to 6 days.

1 cup (250 mL) walnuts, ground

6 dates, pitted and chopped

½ cup (125 mL) cacao powder

½ tsp (2 mL) pure vanilla extract

Pinch Himalayan crystal salt

1 tbsp (15 mL) water

Ground almonds or hemp seeds,
   shredded coconut or cacao powder
   for coating

~~~~~~~~

power food tip   *Try making these with your kids. They are a lot of fun to prepare. These truffles also make a great guilt-free snack you can take on the road or to work for a quick energy boost. You could also take some to a house party as a sure way to impress, or give them as a gift to someone special.*

BEETS
BLACK GINGER ALMONDS
BEANS amaranth
vegetables
chickpeas GARLIC BROWN
BLUEBERRIES
seeds fruits PISTACHIOS RICE
GOJI PECANS AVOCADOS GREEN PEAS
nuts
BERRIES grains
WHOLE OATS CASHEWS
QUINOA KALE LENTILS
COCONUT
legumes

THE POWER OF FLAXSEEDS

WHY YOU SHOULD CARE Do you or someone you know have trouble with constipation? How about gas or bloating? Do you want it to go away? Ground flax along with proper hydration is your key to gaining a healthier gut flora and avoiding internal inflammation. The more your body stores toxins and spends energy trying to eliminate waste, the weaker your immune system becomes. It is that simple. Want to stay alive longer? Eating this very powerful seed will help you do just that.

HOW TO USE Flaxseeds, like most other seeds, can be eaten in their whole state once shelled, no heating required. However, whole flaxseeds tend to slip through your intestines without providing their full benefit, because they are a very small and slippery seed. Flaxseeds are best consumed ground, allowing for all their health benefits to be released and enhancing their nutrient absorption.

Breakfast: Sprinkle 1 to 2 tbsp (15 to 30 mL) ground flaxseeds into your cereal, smoothie or baked goods such as muffins and breads.

Lunch/Snack: Grind 2 tbsp (30 mL) flaxseeds and spread in the middle of your next sandwich or wrap, or mix into a soup or salad. Just add a little to feel the power of better digestion.

Dinner: Grind some flaxseeds and add the flour to veggie burgers, sprinkle over steamed vegetables or mix into whatever you are eating tonight. Be sure to drink a nice big glass of water 1 hour after your meal to help flush your system and keep your energy sustained long term.

HOW TO STORE Flaxseeds are a great source of omega-3 and omega-6 essential fatty acids. They should therefore be stored in the refrigerator (for up to 3 months when ground) or in the freezer (for up to 6 months). Be sure to keep a jar of ground flaxseeds in the door of your refrigerator for quick access, right beside your hemp seeds and almonds.

> *There is so much nutritional value in this little seed shaped like a teardrop. Flax is like the toothbrush of your intestines, cleansing you of unwanted toxins. Flaxseed is best if ground to help release the soluble and insoluble forms of fibre. Once flax is ground, the essential fatty acid content coupled with a strong dose of fibre makes flaxseeds a powerful addition to your daily diet.*

BANANA FLAX JACKS

MAKES 6 PANCAKES

IN A LARGE BOWL, combine and mix all the dry ingredients. In a separate bowl, combine the egg and milk. Add the wet ingredients to the dry ingredients and mix. In a non-stick frying pan over medium heat, place 1 tsp (5 mL) of the coconut oil. Pour a hand-size amount of batter into the pan for each pancake. Press a few slices of the banana into the top of each pancake. Flip your pancakes when the underside is golden brown. Serve immediately, garnished with the rest of your banana and some chopped almonds, if desired.

~~~~~~

power food tip *Any leftovers are great as a snack for work or play. Try spreading some almond butter or applesauce overtop for a healthy snack.*

¼ cup (60 mL) flaxseeds, ground

1 tbsp (15 mL) flaxseeds, whole

1½ cups (375 mL) buckwheat flour

1 tbsp (15 mL) coconut sugar

2 tsp (10 mL) baking powder

½ tsp (2 mL) baking soda

1 tsp (5 mL) cinnamon

¼ tsp (1 mL) Himalayan crystal salt

1 egg

1 cup (250 mL) hemp milk (page 81)

Coconut oil for frying

1 banana, thinly sliced

POWER DATE BARS

MAKES 10 BARS

CHOP THE DATES in half to ensure they contain no pits. Place the chopped dates into a food processor with the water and blend for a few seconds. Add all the remaining ingredients and blend together. Line an 8-inch (20 cm) square baking dish with waxed paper or parchment paper. Spread the mixture evenly in the pan about 1 inch (2.5 cm) thick, to be cut into bars once hardened. Refrigerate overnight. Cut into 10 bars and freeze in an airtight glass container, to be eaten as desired.

~~~~~~

power food tip *Try turning these into a cereal bar by adding 1 cup (250 mL) quinoa flakes to the mix.*

2 cups (500 mL) pitted dates, chopped

2 tbsp (30 mL) water

½ cup (125 mL) flaxseeds, ground

¼ cup (60 mL) sesame seeds, ground

¼ cup (60 mL) sunflower seeds, ground

¼ cup (60 mL) hemp seeds

¼ cup (60 mL) shredded coconut

ONLINE BONUS

Visit PowerofFood.com to watch a video on how to make these bars.

THE POWER OF HEMP SEEDS

WHY YOU SHOULD CARE If you know my work, you know hemp seeds are the one Power Food I talk about most, because they are truly a gift from Mother Nature. I encourage you to eat 4 to 6 tbsp (60 to 90 mL) daily. If you want sustained energy all day long without needing to change your diet in any way, this is the food for you. Before you eat your next cookie or piece of cake, eat 1 tbsp (15 mL) hemp seeds and then enjoy your cake. *Why are you telling me it's okay to eat cookies and cake, Adam?* By eating something with nutritional value along with something *without* any nutritional value, you are now getting something rather then nothing. Just by adding in 1 tbsp (15 mL) hemp seeds to everything you eat, you will automatically help control your blood sugar and avoid the dreaded daily cycle of energy highs and lows.

HOW TO USE Hemp seeds have a great nutty taste and are ideal when eaten in their whole state once shelled. Unlike flaxseeds, hemp seeds do not need to be ground to impart all their nutritional value. I go through 5 lb (2.2 kg) a month by adding them into my daily meals whole or by making a daily batch of hemp milk, hemp butter or hemp flour. You can also find hemp oil, which is a great addition to salad dressings, dips and soups. Look at it this way: if you still have the same hemp seeds in the refrigerator longer than 2 weeks, you need to start adding them to everything you eat. That is how vital they are to powering up your energy levels throughout your day.

Breakfast: Sprinkle 2 tbsp (30 mL) into your cereal, oatmeal or smoothie, or add a handful on top of your next plate of pancakes. A nice glass of hemp milk also makes a great morning nutritional boost.

Lunch/Snack: Add 2 tbsp (30 mL) hemp seeds or hemp oil into your soups, salads, sandwiches, wraps or dips.

Dinner: Add ¼ cup (60 mL) hemp seeds to your stews, pasta dishes and stir-fries. Sprinkle them over steamed vegetables. Just add them to your dinner tonight to help eliminate your late-night sugar cravings. Yes, I know all about your late-night cravings. I once had them too.

HOW TO STORE Like most nuts and seeds, due to their high essential fatty acid content, hemp seeds are best kept in the refrigerator (for up to 3 months) or in the freezer (for up to 6 months). Keep a jar of hemp seeds in the door of your refrigerator for quick access, right beside your ground flaxseeds and almonds.

Hemp seeds, also known as hemp hearts—which look a little like sesame seeds but are rounder, greener and softer—are one of the world's most balanced and complete foods. If there is any single food to start including in your daily diet, this is it. Hemp seeds are a complete source of protein, they contain all the essential fatty acids, and they are an abundant source of vitamins, minerals and antioxidants. Hemp is also suitable for those unable to eat gluten, sugar, milk, nuts or meat.

HEMPTASTIC CRACKERS

MAKES 12 BITE-SIZE CRACKERS

PLACE ALL THE INGREDIENTS into a food processor and blend until smooth. Once blended, spread the batter evenly onto a dehydrator tray or large baking sheet covered with parchment paper or waxed paper. Dehydrate at 105°F (41°C) for 24 hours, flipping your cracker after 12 hours. If using an oven, bake at the lowest temperature for 30 to 45 minutes. If the cracker is still moist after baking, flip it over and bake for another 30 minutes, or until it reaches your desired crispiness. Once done, break your cracker into bite-size pieces to enjoy as desired. Store your crackers in an airtight glass container and freeze them for up to 6 months as a great on-the-go snack.

power food tip   *These crackers are delicious crumbled into a bowl of soup or overtop of a salad to give it some extra crunch. Go for it!*

1½ cups (375 mL) hemp seeds

1 cup (250 mL) chia seeds

1 cup (250 mL) flaxseeds, ground

2 cups (500 mL) artichoke hearts

1 beet, chopped

1 tomato, diced

1 onion, diced

1 clove garlic, minced

½ cup (125 mL) parsley, chopped

¼ cup (60 mL) water

Juice of 1 lemon

1 tsp (5 mL) grated ginger

1 tbsp (15 mL) prepared mustard

1 tsp (5 mL) Himalayan crystal salt

1 tsp (5 mL) ground black pepper

JUST DO IT HEMP MILK

MAKES 4 CUPS (1 L)

PLACE THE INGREDIENTS into a blender and blend until smooth. Your power drink is now ready to serve. I use hemp milk as the base of most of my smoothies, for my cream-based soups, for dips and spreads as well as for my yummy Easy Grain Risotto (page 106). Store in an airtight glass jar in the refrigerator and consume within 2 to 3 days.

1 cup (250 mL) hemp seeds

3 cups (750 mL) water

Pictured on facing page.

power food tip *Feel free to add a combination of 1 tsp (5 mL) pure vanilla extract, ½ tsp (2 mL) ground cinnamon, ¼ cup (60 mL) chopped dates or 1 tbsp (15 mL) maple syrup to create the taste you desire.*

IRON PUMPING RECOVERY DRINK

MAKES 4 CUPS (1 L)

PLACE ALL THE INGREDIENTS into a blender and blend. It is that easy! Store your drink in an airtight glass jar in the refrigerator and consume within 24 hours.

1 cup (250 mL) hemp seeds

½ cup (125 mL) blueberries

¼ cup (60 mL) chia seeds

¼ cup (60 mL) dried goji berries

1 banana

3 cups (750 mL) water

power food tip *Add 1 tbsp (15 mL) cacao powder to turn this into a powerful chocolate elixir.*

OPTIMAL ATHLETE'S GRANOLA

MAKES 4 CUPS (1 L)

PLACE ALL THE INGREDIENTS into a large mixing bowl and mix together using a spatula. Spread the cereal onto dehydrator trays. Use 2 or 3 trays to be sure to spread out the cereal evenly for optimal drying. Dehydrate at 105°F (41°C) for 12 hours. If using an oven, spread the granola over a large baking sheet and bake at the lowest temperature for 20 minutes. Continue baking as needed until all the moisture is removed. Store your granola in an airtight glass container in the cupboard. It will keep for 14 days.

power food tip *I like to double this recipe to ensure I always have enough on hand for snacking or for enjoying before a big day of rock climbing or ski touring.*

2 cups (500 mL) buckwheat
1 cup (250 mL) hemp seeds
½ cup (125 mL) chia seeds
½ cup (125 mL) honey
¼ cup (60 mL) molasses
¼ cup (60 mL) raisins
¼ cup (60 mL) dried goji berries
1 tbsp (15 mL) vanilla powder
1 tbsp (15 mL) cinnamon

FLOURLESS HEMP PEANUT BUTTER COOKIES

MAKES 8–12 COOKIES

PREHEAT THE OVEN to 350°F (180°C). Line a large baking sheet with parchment paper. In a large mixing bowl, combine all the ingredients. Spoon out small ball–size portions and flatten them onto the parchment paper with a fork. Bake until golden brown, 10 to 15 minutes. These cookies are so tasty and so nutritious, and kids love them! Store your cookies in an airtight glass container in the refrigerator and consume within 7 days.

1 cup (250 mL) hemp seeds
¼ cup (60 mL) raw cane sugar
2 eggs
1 cup (250 mL) peanut butter
½ tsp (2 mL) baking soda
¼ cup (60 mL) chocolate chips

power food tip *Add ½ tsp (2 mL) each of cinnamon, nutmeg, allspice and pure vanilla extract to add variety and flavour to your cookies.*

HEMPKIN SEED PIE

MAKES ONE 10-INCH (25 CM) PIE

CRUST Soak the buckwheat in 2 cups (500 mL) water overnight. The next morning, drain and rinse the buckwheat, discarding the water. Place the soaked buckwheat and the remaining crust ingredients into a food processor and blend together. Then spread the crust mixture into a 10-inch (25 cm) pie dish until all edges are covered.

FILLING In 2 separate bowls, soak the hemp seeds and cashews in water for 1 hour. After they have soaked, discard the water and purée the soaked hemp seeds and cashews in a blender with ¼ cup (60 mL) fresh water.

Preheat the oven to 350°F (180°C). If not using canned pumpkin, cut a small pumpkin in half and remove the seeds. Bake the pumpkin halves on a baking sheet in the preheated oven until tender, about 30 to 45 minutes. After the pumpkin has baked, discard the skin. Place the cooked pumpkin flesh or the canned pumpkin with the soaked hemp seeds and cashews and the remaining filling ingredients except the topping into a food processor and blend together. Once it is blended, spread the filling evenly over the crust. Top with 1 to 2 cups (250 to 500 mL) of the Roasted Pumpkin Power Seeds. Refrigerate for 1 hour and then serve. Store leftovers in an airtight glass container in the refrigerator and eat within 3 days.

~~~~~~~~

power food tip *You can replace the buckwheat with soaked chia seeds if you would like a lighter pie crust.*

CRUST

1 cup (250 mL) buckwheat

½ cup (125 mL) almonds, crushed

¼ cup (60 mL) honey

¼ cup (60 mL) shredded coconut

4 pitted dates, chopped

FILLING

1 cup (250 mL) hemp seeds

½ cup (125 mL) cashews

2 cups (500 mL) cooked or canned
   pumpkin

¼ cup (60 mL) maple syrup

1 tsp (5 mL) cinnamon

1 tsp (5 mL) allspice

1 tsp (5 mL) nutmeg

Roasted Pumpkin Power Seeds
   (page 96) for topping

THE POWER OF SESAME SEEDS

WHY YOU SHOULD CARE What is calcium for? How about iron? We know they are good for us, but why? The truth is, we need many vitamins and minerals as well as quality fats, proteins and carbohydrates in order to survive. Each one serves a different purpose. Should you know what each one is and how it fills its role in your body? Not even the best doctors have all those answers, so why should you? All you need to do is ensure you eat the best-quality sources of your required nutrients to meet your daily needs. So what food is a good source of quality iron? How about for your child's calcium intake? It turns out sesame seeds contain over 40% of the recommended daily intake of both calcium and iron. And if you can find them in their unhulled state, with the outer shell intact, you increase the calcium and iron content by another 25%. Who knew? Now you do! This powerful seed is another one of Mother Nature's beautiful little secrets to ensure you have strong bone health and your children grow up well nourished.

HOW TO USE Sesame seeds are great eaten as is. They require no heating and can be added to increase the nutritional value and flavour of every meal you eat. Grind some sesame seeds in a coffee grinder (not used for coffee) to release the essential oils and make them easier to digest. By doing so, you break down the seed, so your digestive system can absorb all those wonderful vitamins and minerals while using up less energy for digestion. This means more energy for you to go out and get active, right?

Breakfast: Sprinkle 2 tbsp (30 mL) ground sesame seeds into your morning cereal, oatmeal or smoothie, or spread some on toast.

Lunch/Snack: Add 2 tbsp (30 mL) ground sesame seeds to your salad or soup. You can even add a handful of whole sesame seeds to your meal to add a nutty taste and a delicate, almost invisible crunch to your meal.

Dinner: Just add some sesame seeds on top of pizza, or to stir-fries, roasted potatoes or a stew. Don't think about it—just do it and feel the power!

HOW TO STORE This is yet another wondrous living food that is best stored in the refrigerator (for no longer then 3 months). Sesame seeds will keep in the freezer for up to 6 months. Keep a jar of ground sesame seeds in the door of your refrigerator for quick access, beside your ground flax, hemp seeds and almonds.

Sesame seeds are not widely recognized for their health benefits, but they pack a powerful punch. In fact, these small, pale-coloured seeds may be the one food most commonly overlooked and tucked away in the back corner of our kitchen cupboards. Well, it is time to pull out the sesame seeds from that sushi order you ate a few months ago and start eating. The combination of fibre, protein and fat found in sesame seeds makes them ideal for human consumption. They also contain a high concentration of magnesium, iron, calcium, zinc, copper and vitamin B in every little seed.

SUPER SESAME PESTO

MAKES 2 CUPS (500 ML)

PLACE ALL THE INGREDIENTS into a food processor and blend together until smooth. You may still have some sesame seeds not crushed, and that is okay. You may need to add more oil, so use your judgment. Serve over a bowl of gluten-free brown rice pasta, or use as a nutty dip for vegetables.

~~~~~~~~

power food tip *Replace 1 tbsp (15 mL) of the olive oil with 1 tbsp (15 mL) hemp oil or flax oil to increase the flavour and omega-3 value of this pesto.*

2 cups (500 mL) basil, chopped and
  packed down
¼ cup (60 mL) pecans, crushed
2 tbsp (30 mL) sesame seeds
1 tbsp (15 mL) tahini
1 clove garlic, minced
2 tbsp (30 mL) extra virgin olive oil
½ tsp (2 mL) lemon juice
¼ tsp (1 mL) Himalayan crystal salt

HEAVENLY HALVAH

MAKES 12 PIECES

IN A LARGE MIXING BOWL, combine all the ingredients except the topping. Line an 8-inch (20 cm) square baking dish with waxed paper or parchment paper. Place the mixture into the prepared baking dish. Sprinkle some hemp seeds overtop and place the halvah in the refrigerator for 1 hour. Once it has cooled, cut into small square portions and serve. Store your halvah in an airtight glass container in the refrigerator for up to 7 days.

½ cup (125 mL) walnuts, ground

¼ cup (60 mL) sesame seeds, ground

¼ cup (60 mL) hemp seeds

3 tbsp (45 mL) tahini

3 tbsp (45 mL) honey

2 tbsp (30 mL) almond butter

½ tsp (2 mL) Himalayan crystal salt

Extra hemp seeds for sprinkling on top

power food tip *How about adding in your favourite nuts or dried fruit? You can even add 2 tbsp (30 mL) cacao powder to make chocolate halvah.*

THE POWER OF CHIA SEEDS

WHY YOU SHOULD CARE How often do you find yourself holding your breath throughout the day? Once, twice, more then three times? Many of us don't realize we spend most of our day in a tense, stiff, stressed response where our shoulders are tucked in tight and our breath is being held. When you hold in your breath you are starving your cells of the vital oxygen keeping them alive. This allows free radicals to attack your cells, killing them off one by one while leaving you fatigued and vulnerable to weight gain. Chia has a powerful amount of antioxidants packed into every little seed. When you eat chia seeds, the powerful antioxidants fight off free radicals in your body and save your cells while giving you a powerful dose of energy. So next time you catch yourself holding your breath and feeling tense in your shoulders, take a long deep breath and eat a handful of chia seeds. Your cells will thank you by providing you with more energy.

HOW TO USE Chia seeds are a truly astounding seed when it comes to recipe creation. They expand 9 to 1 when added to water, which means you can add a couple of tablespoons to any smoothie you make, turning it into an instant pudding. Wait for 5 minutes and watch each little seed expand. Ideally you should consume chia seeds without heating them. I add some to soups and stews after they are cooked to benefit from their nutritional factors as well as to thicken my creations when desired.

Breakfast: Sprinkle 2 tbsp (30 mL) into your cereal, oatmeal or smoothie, or on top of your morning toast.

Lunch/Snack: As with all seeds, you need only add chia seeds to enjoy their health benefits. Try sprinkling 1 tbsp (15 mL) in your sandwich, inside a wrap, into your soup or over a salad.

Dinner: Add chia seeds into your mashed potatoes or mix some with your brown rice. All you have to do is add them to feel their power!

HOW TO STORE Storing chia seeds in the refrigerator is ideal. They will keep fresh for 3 months. If you place them in the freezer you have up to 6 months to use them. It is a good idea to store a little jar of chia seeds in the door of the refrigerator for quick access, beside your ground sesame seeds and flaxseeds, almonds and hemp seeds.

If you are thinking that chia seeds are also the novelty item Chia Pet popular in the 1980s, you would be correct. They are one and the same. So why does chia make my list of most powerful seeds? This versatile little powerhouse—its spotted appearance ranges from white to brown to black—is full of magnesium, calcium, iron and omega-3 essential fatty acids. Native to southern Mexico, chia seeds have recently become so popular, they are in high demand all over North America.

CHIA CHOCOLATE CHERRY LOVE BREAD

MAKES 8 SLICES

PLACE ALL THE INGREDIENTS, except the cacao nibs and walnuts, into a food processor and blend together until the mixture reaches a cake batter consistency. Place the mixture into a large mixing bowl and add the cacao nibs and walnuts. Mix together and then place the dough onto a cutting board. Using your hands, shape the dough into the size of loaf you desire. Next, using a bread knife, slice the loaf into even-size pieces, about 8 slices in total. Spread out the slices on a dehydrator tray. The thicker the slices, the longer they will take to dehydrate or bake. Dehydrate at 105°F (41°C) for 6 hours. Flip over the slices and dehydrate for another 6 hours. If using an oven, bake at the lowest temperature for 30 minutes on one side and 30 minutes on the other. If after the specified time the bread is still too moist, bake or dehydrate longer as needed. Store your bread in an airtight glass container and consume within 4 days, You can freeze your bread to eat as an on-the-go snack; it will keep for up to 3 months frozen.

2 cups (500 mL) chia seeds, ground

1 cup (250 mL) almonds, ground

1 cup (250 mL) hemp seeds

½ cup (125 mL) dried cherries

2 bananas

1 tbsp (15 mL) honey

1 tbsp (15 mL) pure vanilla extract

1 cup (250 mL) hemp milk (page 81)

1 cup (250 mL) cacao nibs

¼ cup (60 mL) walnuts, chopped

~~~~~~~~

power food tip *I sometimes mash a banana and spread a little over each piece before baking. This bread is one I take with me on my multi-day mountain trips. Eating a slice is a great way to recover after a heavy workout.*

VANILLA CREAM COOKIES

MAKES 15 COOKIES

COOKIE Place all the cookie ingredients into a food processor and blend until the mixture turns into dough. Using your hands, create cookie-size shapes from your dough, and lay each one out on a dehydrator tray or on a large baking dish lined with waxed paper or parchment paper.

CREAM Place all the cream ingredients, except the garnish, into a food processor and blend together. Spread some cream evenly over the top of each cookie and garnish with a few whole goji berries. Dehydrate at 105°F (41°C) for 24 hours. Flip over the cookies and dehydrate for another 24 hours. If using an oven, bake at the lowest temperature for 30 minutes on one side and 15 minutes on the other. Bake longer if you desire a crunchier cookie. Store your cookies in an airtight glass container in the refrigerator and eat within 4 to 6 days. You can freeze these to eat as an on-the-go snack; these cookies will keep for up to 3 months frozen.

~~~~~~~

power food tip Add 2 tbsp (30 mL) cacao powder to either your cookie or cream mix to create a chocolate version of this yummy and healthy treat.

COOKIE
½ cup (125 mL) chia seeds
½ cup (125 mL) buckwheat
¼ cup (60 mL) flaxseeds
¼ cup (60 mL) pumpkin seeds
¼ cup (60 mL) sunflower seeds
¼ cup (60 mL) sesame seeds
½ cup (125 mL) raisins
1 cup (250 mL) shredded coconut
½ cup (125 mL) walnuts
½ cup (125 mL) almonds
1 tbsp (15 mL) pure vanilla extract
1 tsp (5 mL) cinnamon
½ cup (125 mL) honey
1 cup (250 mL) water

CREAM
1 banana
1 cup (250 mL) hemp seeds
1 tbsp (15 mL) pure vanilla extract
1 tsp (5 mL) cinnamon
½ cup (125 mL) whole goji berries
  for garnish

GOJI CHIA JERKY

MAKES 12 PIECES

SOAK THE GOJI BERRIES for 20 minutes in 4 cups (1 L) water. Once the goji berries are a little plump, drain them, reserving the water. Place the soaked goji berries and the remaining ingredients (except the berry water) into a food processor and blend together. Add ¼ cup (60 mL) of the reserved goji berry water to the mix as needed until it reaches a runny batter consistency. Spread the batter evenly onto a dehydrator tray or large baking sheet.

Dehydrate at 115°F (46°C) for 6 hours. Flip over the jerky and dehydrate for another 6 hours. Before flipping, if the mixture is still a bit runny, keep dehydrating until the jerky is easy to flip. You want the final texture to be chewy, so do not over-dehydrate.

If using an oven, bake at the lowest temperature for 30 minutes on each side, until the jerky reaches your desired chewiness. When the jerky is done, cut it into strips to your liking. Take a few pieces with you every day while on the go or out for your adventures. Eating Goji Chia Jerky is a great way to stay energized and feel fantastic! Store your jerky in an airtight glass container in the cupboard for up to 2 weeks. If stored in the freezer, it will keep for 3 months.

2 cups (500 mL) whole goji berries
2 cups (500 mL) blueberries
2 cups (500 mL) chia seeds
1 cup (250 mL) hemp seeds
2 tbsp (30 mL) cacao powder
2 tbsp (30 mL) honey
1 tbsp (15 mL) grated ginger
1 tsp (5 mL) cinnamon
½ tsp (2 mL) cayenne pepper
Pinch Himalayan crystal salt

power food tip *Use the same recipe but replace the goji berries with chopped figs. So good.*

PUMPKIN SEED PÂTÉ IN CHARD

MAKES 8 WRAPS

SOAK THE PUMPKIN SEEDS in 2 cups (500 mL) water overnight. The next day, drain and rinse the pumpkin seeds, discarding the water. Place the soaked seeds and the rest of the ingredients (except the chard) in a food processor and blend together. Once the mixture is puréed, place a small scoop into each of the fresh Swiss chard leaves and wrap. Now that's a healthy and delicious meal to impress your family or friends.

~~~~~~

power food tip *Try adding a scoop of Hungry Hungry Hummus (page 120) into a chard leaf for another fantastic wrap alternative.*

1¼ cups (310 mL) pumpkin seeds

¼ cup (60 mL) flax oil or hemp oil

Juice of 1 lemon

¼ cup (60 mL) parsley, chopped

½ tsp (2 mL) grated ginger

¼ cup (60 mL) onion, diced

2 cloves garlic, minced

1 tsp (5 mL) honey

1 tsp (5 mL) cayenne pepper

½ tsp (2 mL) ground black pepper

½ tsp (2 mL) Himalayan crystal salt

8 green Swiss chard leaves for wrapping

Pictured on facing page.

ROASTED PUMPKIN POWER SEEDS

MAKES 4 CUPS (1 L)

IN A MEDIUM SAUCEPAN over medium heat, dry-roast the pumpkin seeds for 2 minutes. Be sure to flip the seeds every 30 seconds. Once the pumpkin seeds have roasted for 2 minutes, add the hemp seeds and maple syrup to the pan. Stir together and continue roasting. Let the maple syrup coat all the seeds. Once all the seeds are coated with the maple syrup, remove from heat and let seeds sit in the pan for 5 minutes. Refrigerate for 20 minutes to harden. Use as a garnish for Hempkin Seed Pie (page 84).

~~~~~~

power food tip *Eat as a snack or add to any of my soup or salad recipes as a nutritional and flavour power boost.*

2 cups (500 mL) pumpkin seeds

1 cup (250 mL) hemp seeds

¼ cup (60 mL) maple syrup

BEETS
BLACK
BEANS
GINGER
amaranth
ALMONDS
vegetables
chickpeas
BLUEBERRIES
GARLIC
AVOCADOS
PISTACHIOS
BROWN
RICE
seeds
fruits
GOJI
PECANS
GREEN PEAS
nuts
BERRIES
grains
WHOLE OATS
QUINOA
COCONUT
KALE
CASHEWS
LENTILS
legumes

THE **POWER** OF **BROWN RICE**

WHY YOU SHOULD CARE Whether it is a friend, co-worker, neighbour or relative, we all seem to know someone with celiac disease, Crohn's disease, colitis or irritable bowel syndrome. Do you yourself suffer from digestive ailments, stomach pain or constant fatigue? If so, finding alternative gluten-free grains will relieve some of your symptoms and allow you to live a more energized life. Brown rice is a perfect grain to fit your needs and a great substitute for wheat in your diet.

HOW TO USE To cook brown rice, for every 1 cup (250 mL) rice, use 2 cups (500 mL) water. Bring to a boil in a small saucepan. Once the rice is boiling, add 1 tsp (5 mL) extra virgin olive oil and a pinch of Himalayan crystal salt. Reduce the heat and simmer covered until tender, about 30 minutes. Stir occasionally. Keep an eye on the rice to ensure it does not burn. Add a little more water if needed. Once the rice is done, fluff with a fork. I like to cook a little extra to have for lunch the next day.

Breakfast: Cook as above and add 1 cup (250 mL) hemp milk (page 81), 1 tsp (5 mL) maple syrup and ¼ cup (60 mL) organic raisins for a powerful breakfast cereal.

Lunch/Snack: Add a handful of cooked brown rice to your salad or soup. Or use brown rice as an alternative to wheat-based wraps.

Dinner: Use brown rice as a nutritional side dish for any number of tasty meals.

HOW TO STORE Uncooked brown rice should be stored in a dark place in an airtight container and keeps for up to 1 year. Once cooked, brown rice should be stored in the refrigerator and consumed within 5 days. I tend to cook 1 cup (250 mL) brown rice each week and store in the refrigerator for quick daily access.

Brown rice—essentially unmilled or partially milled rice, retaining its bran layer and germ—is a great alternative to popular gluten-based grains. A gluten-free grain, brown rice is also a super source of complex carbohydrates, quality protein and several vitamins and minerals. One cup (250 mL) of uncooked brown rice makes about 2 cups (500 mL) of cooked brown rice.

BROWN RICE TORTILLA PIZZA

MAKES TWO 12-INCH (30 CM) PIZZAS

PREHEAT THE OVEN to 350°F (180°C). Brush each wrap with 1 tbsp (15 mL) of the olive oil. In a large mixing bowl, combine all the remaining ingredients, except the cheese, with the remaining 3 tbsp (45 mL) olive oil. Spread the mixture evenly over both wraps. Top each with the shredded cheese. Place your "pizzas" on a baking sheet and bake in the centre of the preheated oven for about 10 minutes, or until the cheese is melted.

~~~~~

power food tip   *Use my Hungry Hungry Hummus recipe (page 120) as a sauce for this pizza (in addition to the olive oil). You will love it!*

2 brown rice wraps

5 tbsp (75 mL) extra virgin olive oil

2 medium tomatoes, diced

1 red pepper, diced

1 onion, diced

4 cloves garlic, minced

1 tsp (5 mL) rosemary, chopped

1 tsp (5 mL) basil, chopped

1 cup (250 mL) shredded cheese
  of your choice

GLUTEN-FREE BROWN RICE WRAP

MAKES 1 WRAP

PLACE ALL THE OTHER INGREDIENTS into the wrap and roll. That's an easy lunch for times when you're on the go.

~~~~~

power food tip   *Get creative with these wraps. Try making a wrap with almond butter and crushed fresh seasonal berries for a quick, healthy lunch or snack.*

1 brown rice wrap

1 tbsp (15 mL) tahini

½ tomato, sliced

1 avocado, peeled, pitted and sliced

Handful of spinach

1 tbsp (15 mL) hemp seeds

2 tbsp (30 mL) almonds, ground

GLUTEN-FREE BANANA BREAD

MAKES ONE 9- × 5-INCH (2 L) LOAF

SOAK THE DATES in ½ cup (125 mL) water for 20 minutes. Once they are softened, in a small mixing bowl, mash the dates with their water until they are a bit mushy, or blend in a food processor. Preheat the oven to 350°F (180°C). In a large mixing bowl, mash the bananas. Add the soaked dates and the remaining ingredients, except the sesame seeds. Once the batter is mixed, place it into a 9- × 5-inch (2 L) loaf pan and top with the sesame seeds. Bake in the preheated oven for 45 to 60 minutes. Test it for doneness with a fork or chopstick to be sure it is cooked right through. Once baked, let it cool, slice and serve with some fresh seasonal berries.

≈≈≈≈≈≈

power food tip *Spread 1 tbsp (15 mL) almond butter overtop before eating. You can even try spreading a slice with some Strawberry Cashew Cream (page 71) if you want to go crazy.*

¾ cup (185 mL) pitted dates, chopped

4 ripe bananas

2½ cups (625 mL) brown rice flour

½ cup (125 mL) water

2 eggs

½ cup (125 mL) walnuts or pecans, chopped

1 tsp (5 mL) baking soda

½ tsp (2 mL) baking powder

½ tsp (2 mL) cinnamon

¼ tsp (1 mL) nutmeg

¼ cup (60 mL) sesame seeds

MACHO MAN LOAF

MAKES ONE 9- × 5-INCH (2 L) LOAF

PREHEAT THE OVEN to 350°F (180°C). Place the red pepper, onion, garlic, ketchup, herbs, egg, olive oil, salt and pepper into a food processor. Blend until smooth. Place the blended mixture into a large mixing bowl. Add the whole and ground sesame seeds and cooked rice, and mix together. Place the mixture into a 9- × 5-inch (2 L) loaf pan. Bake in the preheated oven for 45 minutes. Top it off with Heart-Healthy Gravy (page 128) for the perfect combo. Store any leftovers in an airtight container in the refrigerator for up to 3 days.

~~~~~~

power food tip *Add ¼ cup (60 mL) each of hemp seeds and ground flaxseeds to increase the nutritional punch of this loaf. Why not double the recipe and make two loaves, one for tonight and the other to freeze to enjoy when you need a quick lunch or dinner?*

1 red pepper, diced

1 small onion, diced

2 cloves garlic, minced

½ cup (125 mL) ketchup

¼ cup (60 mL) mixed oregano and
   basil, chopped

1 egg

½ cup (125 mL) extra virgin olive oil

1 tsp (5 mL) Himalayan crystal salt

1 tsp (5 mL) ground black pepper

½ cup (125 mL) sesame seeds, whole

½ cup (125 mL) sesame seeds, ground

1 cup (250 mL) brown rice, cooked

THE POWER OF WHOLE OATS

WHY YOU SHOULD CARE Do you wake up in the morning often wondering what you should eat that will give you sustained energy all day long? Look no further then the power of whole oat groats. Because of its quality carbohydrate content, this grain is the ideal fuel for your breakfast, providing you with a steady stream of energy all day long.

HOW TO USE You can cook whole oat groats the same way as rice, but I prefer to soak them. They are easy to soak, and this ensures you maintain their full nutritional value. Rinse your whole oats thoroughly by running them under fresh water. For every 1 cup (250 mL) whole oat groats you wish to soak, use 2 cups (500 mL) water. Leave them soaking overnight. In the morning, rinse the grains with fresh water and serve. No heating necessary. You can also find steel-cut oats or stone-ground oats, which are the whole oats broken down without using heat, thus preserving their nutritional value. Cook steel-cut or stone-ground oats the same way as whole oat groats or soak them as described.

Breakfast: Sprinkle 2 to 4 tbsp (30 to 60 mL) soaked whole oats into your morning cereal or smoothie. You can even top a few tablespoons with some fresh seasonal fruit and a little natural honey.

Lunch/Snack: Add 2 tbsp (30 mL) into your salad, soup or sandwich.

Dinner: Here is a bonus recipe as an example of how to use this grain in a creative way. Cut off the tops of 2 red peppers and remove the seeds. Place the peppers on a baking sheet and bake at 350°F (180°C) for 15 minutes. Once they are baked, stuff the peppers with a mixture of soaked whole oat groats, ground almonds and some dried cranberries. Get creative with your grains at dinner to enjoy a burst of energy with every bite.

HOW TO STORE Uncooked whole oat groats can be stored in a dark place in an airtight container for up to 1 year. Once cooked, whole oat groats should be stored in the refrigerator and consumed within 5 days. I tend to prepare 1 cup (250 mL) per week and store it in the refrigerator so I can easily add it daily to the foods I love to eat.

Whole oat groats, which are oats in their least processed form, are a great source of fibre, complex carbohydrates, calcium and phosphorous as well as a source of high-quality protein. One cup (250 mL) of uncooked whole oat groats makes about 2 cups (500 mL) of cooked whole oat groats.

RISE AND SHINE CEREAL

MAKES 2 CUPS (500 ML)

PLACE ALL THE INGREDIENTS into a bowl, and enjoy a breakfast that will give you instant and long-lasting energy.

〜〜〜

power food tip *Take the same recipe (without the honey and milk) in a container to work and enjoy as a snack or for lunch.*

1 cup (250 mL) whole oat groats, cooked or soaked

1 tbsp (15 mL) flaxseeds, ground

1 tbsp (15 mL) hemp seeds

1 tbsp (15 mL) sunflower seeds

1 tbsp (15 mL) sesame seeds, ground

1 tbsp (15 mL) raisins or dried cranberries

1 tsp (5 mL) honey

1 cup (250 mL) hemp milk (page 81)

JUMP-START GRANOLA

MAKES 4 CUPS (1 L)

PREHEAT THE OVEN to 300°F (150°C). In a medium bowl, place all the ingredients except the honey and apple juice. In a separate bowl, blend the honey and apple juice until the mixture is smooth in texture. Add the liquid mixture to the dry ingredients and mix well. Spread the mixture onto a large baking sheet. Bake in the preheated oven for 40 minutes. Let your granola cool and then break it up into pieces as you like. Store in an airtight glass container in the cupboard for up to 2 weeks.

〜〜〜

power food tip *Add any number of organic dried fruits to increase the flavour and sweetness of this granola. Even better would be to top off your bowl of granola with some fresh seasonal berries.*

½ cup (125 mL) steel-cut oats, cooked or soaked

½ cup (125 mL) quinoa, cooked

1 cup (250 mL) sunflower seeds

½ cup (125 mL) sesame seeds, ground

1½ tsp (7 mL) cinnamon

¼ tsp (1 mL) nutmeg

¼ tsp (1 mL) Himalayan crystal salt

¼ cup (60 mL) honey

2 tbsp (30 mL) apple juice

EASY GRAIN RISOTTO

MAKES 4 CUPS (1 L)

IN A MEDIUM SAUCEPAN over medium heat, sauté the onion and garlic in 1 tbsp (15 mL) of the coconut oil for 2 minutes. Add the whole oat groats and quinoa. Cook and stir for 2 more minutes. Stir in the hemp milk, salt and pepper, herbs and remaining 2 tbsp (30 mL) of coconut oil. Bring the mixture to a boil, reduce heat and simmer covered for 15 to 20 minutes. Stir your risotto every few minutes to ensure the bottom does not overcook. When done the risotto should be a little creamy. If necessary, add in a little more hemp milk and coconut oil until the mixture reaches your desired consistency. For the final touch, garnish with about 1 tbsp (15 mL) each of the hemp seeds and ground almonds.

power food tip *Make double the amount to have leftovers for lunch tomorrow. Try using amaranth or millet to replace either the quinoa or whole oat groats to create a different style of risotto.*

1 medium onion, diced

2 cloves garlic, minced

3 tbsp (45 mL) coconut oil

1 cup (250 mL) whole oat groats, cooked or soaked

1 cup (250 mL) quinoa, cooked

2 cups (500 mL) hemp milk (page 81)

1 tsp (5 mL) Himalayan crystal salt

1 tsp (5 mL) ground black pepper

2 tbsp (30 mL) fresh herbs, chopped

Hemp seeds and ground almonds for garnish

THE POWER OF AMARANTH

WHY YOU SHOULD CARE Any food that has been classified as a "Food of Immortals" is one I want to eat. That is what the Aztecs called amaranth. Would you like to live a long and vibrant life? Including this powerful grain in your daily diet will ensure your muscles stay strong and your energy high.

HOW TO USE Amaranth cooks very quickly, making it an ideal choice if you need to eat something quick and want more energy. It only takes about 10 minutes to prepare. Place equal amounts of amaranth and water or nut/seed milk in a saucepan and bring to a boil. Reduce heat and simmer covered for 5 to 8 minutes.

Breakfast: Add cooked amaranth to your cereal. You can even add a little when baking your favourite muffin or cookie recipe or homemade bread. I like to use it in my smoothies as a thickener as well.

Lunch/Snack: Amaranth is great for a lunchtime boost. Just add a couple of tablespoons of cooked amaranth to your salad or soup. You can even mix it with hemp seeds to create a nutritional power meal to fuel you for the rest of the day.

Dinner: The dinner options are endless with amaranth. Just add a few tablespoons to whatever you are eating. Amaranth can also be used as filler when preparing veggie burgers or eaten instead of rice under a stir-fry.

HOW TO STORE Uncooked amaranth can be stored in a dark place in an airtight container for up to 8 months. Once cooked, any leftover amaranth should be stored in the refrigerator and consumed within 5 days. Try taking a cup of cooked amaranth to work as a healthy snack for a quick energy boost.

Tiny cream-coloured seeds categorized as a grain, amaranth is a super Power Food. For every grain of amaranth that enters your mouth, you are supplying your body with a large dose of high-quality protein and complex carbohydrates as well as a large amount of calcium and iron. Amaranth is definitely a whole food to include in your diet as frequently as possible. One cup (250 mL) of uncooked amaranth makes about 2 cups (500 mL) of cooked amaranth.

AMARANTH TABBOULEH

MAKES 3 CUPS (750 ML)

PLACE ALL THE INGREDIENTS except the olives into a large mixing bowl and gently mix together. Place your tabbouleh into the freezer for 5 minutes to chill before serving. Garnish with the diced olives.

~~~~~~~~

power food tip *Serve your tabbouleh over one of my fresh vegetable crackers, such as Hemptastic Crackers (page 79).*

2 cups (500 mL) amaranth, cooked

1 cup (250 mL) hemp milk (page 81)

½ green onion, diced

2 cloves garlic, minced

1 cup (250 mL) parsley, chopped

2 tbsp (30 mL) mint, chopped

½ cup (125 mL) lemon juice

¼ cup (60 mL) extra virgin olive oil

2 tbsp (30 mL) black and green olives, diced, for garnish

AMARANTH-STUFFED SQUASH

MAKES 2 SERVINGS

PREHEAT THE OVEN to 350°F (180°C). Cut the squash in half and remove the seeds. With the tines of a fork, make small holes in the flesh of each squash half. In a small mixing bowl, mix together the olive oil, lemon juice and mustard. Pour this mixture into the holes of the squash. Place the squash halves cut side up on a baking sheet and bake in the preheated oven for 45 minutes, or until fork tender.

STUFFING In a mixing bowl, combine all the stuffing ingredients. Stuff each cooked squash half until full.

~~~~~~~

power food tip *Replace the amaranth with cooked brown rice or quinoa to create different gluten-free stuffing options.*

1 butternut squash
¼ cup (60 mL) extra virgin olive oil
Juice of ½ lemon
1 tsp (5 mL) prepared mustard

STUFFING

2 cups (500 mL) amaranth, cooked
½ cup (125 mL) sunflower seeds, whole
¼ cup (60 mL) sunflower seeds, ground
1 tbsp (15 mL) each flaxseeds, hemp seeds and sesame seeds
2 tbsp (30 mL) basil, chopped
¼ cup (60 mL) dried cranberries

THE POWER OF QUINOA

WHY YOU SHOULD CARE Do you often come home after a long day at work and wonder what to make for dinner? Is it going to be another night of macaroni and cheese, or is today going to be the day you turn it up a notch? Quinoa is your secret weapon for those long days when you desire something quick and easy to make that will leave you feeling fantastic. Eating 1 to 2 cups (250 to 500 mL) cooked quinoa about 4 hours before bed is the ideal way to ensure you have a comfortable, restful sleep.

HOW TO USE Rinse quinoa thoroughly by running it under fresh water. For every 1 cup (250 mL) quinoa, use 2 cups (500 mL) water. Cook quinoa the same way you cook rice. You can also soak quinoa and sprout it for a healthier way to consume it. Sprouting releases the digestive enzymes, making it even easier for you to digest. And easier digestion means more energy for you. Watch a video on how to sprout quinoa at PowerofFood.com.

Breakfast: Sprinkle 2 tbsp (30 mL) cooked or sprouted quinoa into your cereal or smoothie, or add some on top of your morning toast.

Lunch/Snack: I often take ⅓ cup (80 mL) cooked or sprouted quinoa on the road with me to add it to the foods I will eat for the day. This way I don't have to stress about eating healthy all the time; I just add the health without restrictions. Along with adding some key seeds such as hemp seeds, adding a few tablespoons of quinoa goes a long way toward keeping you energized.

Dinner: Place ½ cup (125 mL) quinoa on a plate with vegetables of your choice and enjoy a very nourishing meal. Try eating with your next stir-fry. Or add some to a salad or on top of the next pizza you order in.

HOW TO STORE Uncooked quinoa can be stored in a dark place in an airtight container for up to 1 year. Once cooked or sprouted, quinoa should be stored in the refrigerator and consumed within 5 days.

A tiny seed that can be found in white, red or black varieties, quinoa is a great source of fibre, complex carbohydrates, calcium, phosphorous, iron and vitamins B and E. If that weren't enough, what makes quinoa so special is its protein content. Quinoa is a superb way to consume digestible protein. It is a complete protein, containing all the essential amino acids, and is great if you are gluten intolerant. One cup (250 mL) of uncooked quinoa makes about 2 cups (500 mL) of cooked quinoa.

QUINOA VANILLA PUDDING

MAKES 8 SERVINGS

PLACE THE WATER, hemp seeds, cinnamon and vanilla into a blender and mix to create hemp milk. In a medium saucepan over medium heat, place the prepared hemp milk, quinoa, goji berries and salt, and bring to a quick boil. Reduce heat and simmer covered until most of the liquid is absorbed and the quinoa is soft, not grainy. If it is not soft, add a little water and continue cooking. Be sure to stir often to avoid burning the quinoa. Once the quinoa is ready, add the maple syrup or coconut sugar and coconut oil. Serve topped with the chopped almonds. Store any leftovers in an airtight glass container in the refrigerator for up to 3 days.

power food tip *Feel free to replace the quinoa with amaranth or any other gluten-free grain, such as brown rice, to create some variety in your pudding.*

4½ cups (1 L + 125 mL) water
½ cup (125 mL) hemp seeds
1 tsp (5 mL) cinnamon
1 tsp (5 mL) pure vanilla extract
2 cups (500 mL) quinoa
½ cup (125 mL) dried goji berries
  or raisins
Pinch Himalayan crystal salt
3 tbsp (45 mL) maple syrup or
  coconut sugar
2 tbsp (30 mL) coconut oil
Chopped almonds for garnish

SPRING QUINOA SALAD

MAKES 4 CUPS (1 L)

PLACE ALL THE INGREDIENTS into a large mixing bowl and gently mix together. Garnish with some hemp seeds.

power food tip *Make the same salad, but replace the quinoa with another nutritious grain, such as amaranth or whole oat groats, for variety and to benefit from more whole grains in your diet.*

2 cups (500 mL) quinoa, cooked
1 cup (250 mL) sunflower seeds
1 red pepper, diced
¼ cup (60 mL) raisins
¼ cup (60 mL) sesame oil
2 tbsp (30 mL) balsamic vinegar
1 tbsp (15 mL) lemon juice
½ tsp (2 mL) Himalayan crystal salt
½ tsp (2 mL) ground black pepper
Hemp seeds for garnish

QUINOA GREEK SALAD

MAKES 4 CUPS (1 L)

PLACE THE DICED, bite-size pieces of tomatoes, cucumber, red pepper, onion and olives in a large mixing bowl and add the garlic, basil, salt and pepper. Next add the cooked quinoa, olive oil, vinegar, lemon juice, hemp seeds, sunflower seeds and raisins. Gently stir together to combine all the ingredients. Crumble the organic feta over the top and serve.

≈≈≈≈≈

power food tip *Try replacing the raisins with ½ cup (125 mL) fresh local seasonal berries for a vibrant take on this salad.*

¾ cup (185 mL) cherry tomatoes, diced

1 cucumber, diced

½ red pepper, diced

½ red onion, diced

¼ cup (60 mL) black or green olives, diced

2 cloves garlic, minced

¼ cup (60 mL) basil, chopped

½ tsp (2 mL) Himalayan crystal salt

½ tsp (2 mL) ground black pepper

2 cups (500 mL) quinoa, cooked

3 tbsp (45 mL) extra virgin olive oil

2 tbsp (30 mL) balsamic vinegar

1 tbsp (15 mL) lemon juice

1 tbsp (15 mL) hemp seeds

1 tbsp (15 mL) sunflower seeds

¼ cup (60 mL) raisins

¼ cup (60 mL) feta

COCONUT QUINOA CURRY

MAKES 8 TO 12 SERVINGS

IN A MEDIUM SAUCEPAN, cook the diced potatoes and sweet potatoes in boiling water until tender, about 15 minutes. In a separate saucepan, bring the 1 cup (250 mL) quinoa to a boil in 2 cups (500 mL) water. Reduce heat and simmer covered for 10 minutes. Meanwhile, place all the remaining ingredients into a large pot and simmer for 20 minutes. Add the cooked quinoa and potatoes to the large pot and continue to simmer for an additional 10 minutes. Keep stirring your curry throughout the cooking process. Store any leftovers in an airtight glass container in the refrigerator for up to 3 days.

~~~~~~

power food tip *Garnish each bowl with some freshly ground cashews for extra flavour and a nutritional boost.*

3 potatoes, diced

3 sweet potatoes, diced

1 cup (250 mL) quinoa

1 can (14 oz/398 mL) coconut milk

3 cups (750 mL) water

Juice of ½ lemon

1 large tomato, diced

½ zucchini, diced

½ broccoli, diced

1 cup (250 mL) spinach

1 can (14 oz/398 mL) corn

1 mango, peeled, pitted and diced

1 large onion, diced

4 cloves garlic, chopped

2 tbsp (30 mL) each cilantro, basil and rosemary, chopped

1 tbsp (15 mL) prepared mustard

2 tbsp (30 mL) grated ginger

2 tbsp (30 mL) curry powder

½ tsp (2 mL) Himalayan crystal salt

½ tsp (2 mL) ground black pepper

ONLINE BONUS

Visit PowerofFood.com to watch a video on how to prepare this recipe.

START YOUR ENGINES SMOOTHIE

MAKES 3 CUPS (750 ML)

PLACE ALL THE INGREDIENTS into a blender and blend. Add more water as needed until the mixture reaches your desired consistency.

~~~~~~

power food tip *Try making double the amount and having the second portion for lunch or a snack.*

¼ cup (60 mL) quinoa, cooked

2 tbsp (30 mL) hemp seeds

½ cup (125 mL) fruit (any seasonal berries)

2 cups (500 mL) water

CHOCOLATE POPCORN

MAKES 1 LARGE PARTY BOWL, ABOUT 10 CUPS (2.5 L)

PLACE THE OIL in a large pot with a lid. Add the popcorn kernels and put on the lid. Over medium heat, shake the pan while holding it close to the burner, but not directly on top. Keeping the steam inside the pot is the key to making great popcorn. Within 5 minutes the kernels of corn will begin to pop. Keep shaking, with the lid held on tight to keep the steam in to pop the kernels. In a medium saucepan over medium heat, melt the chocolate with the hemp milk and salt. After the corn has popped and the chocolate has melted, in a large mixing bowl, pour the melted chocolate over the hot popped corn and mix together until each piece is coated. Place your chocolate popcorn in the freezer for 10 minutes to harden the chocolate.

~~~~~~

power food tip *Enhance the nutritional value of this snack by mixing hemp seeds in with the chocolate before coating your popcorn.*

1 tbsp (15 mL) extra virgin olive oil

1 cup (250 mL) popcorn

½ cup (125 mL) chocolate

2 tbsp (30 mL) hemp milk (page 81)

1 tsp (5 mL) Himalayan crystal salt

BEETS BLACK GINGER ALMONDS
BEANS amaranth
vegetables
chickpeas BLUEBERRIES GARLIC AVOCADOS PISTACHIOS BROWN
RICE
seeds fruits
GOJI PECANS GREEN PEAS
nuts
BERRIES grains
WHOLE OATS KALE CASHEWS
QUINOA LENTILS
COCONUT
legumes

THE POWER OF CHICKPEAS

WHY YOU SHOULD CARE "Beans, beans, are good for your heart / The more you eat, the more you. . ." I'll let you fill in the blank on that one. Do you remember singing that as a child? I sure do, and it turns out it was true. I'm talking about the *good for your heart* part. Have you ever experienced tightness in your chest? Do you know someone who has suffered from a heart attack—perhaps a loved one? What a scary thought to have your heart all of a sudden stop pumping. Well, the great news is that chickpeas help reduce your chances of getting heart disease due to their amazing fibre content. Eating more fibre on a daily basis keeps toxins flowing through your digestive system and ensures no unwanted waste builds up in your precious arteries.

HOW TO USE Chickpeas can be found as a flour, but most are consumed in their whole state. If you are using canned chickpeas, rinse them off under running water before eating, which will remove much of the added salt and oils. If using dried chickpeas, soak them for 4 to 6 hours before cooking. This helps reduce the cooking time. Once they have soaked, drain the chickpeas and rinse them well. Next place the chickpeas into a saucepan of fresh water and bring it to a boil. Reduce the heat and simmer uncovered until the beans are soft all the way through, about 45 minutes. Once they are cooked, drain, rinse and store in the refrigerator in an airtight glass container for 3 to 4 days.

Breakfast: Try adding ¼ cup (60 mL) chickpea flour to replace ¼ cup (60 mL) of your regular flour in any baking recipe or pancakes.

Lunch/Snack: During your next lunch, add ¼ cup (60 mL) chickpeas directly into your soup or salad. You can even spread a little Hungry Hungry Hummus (page 120) on a piece of kale or spinach for a healthy kick to your afternoon.

Dinner: Chickpeas make a fine addition to vegetable burgers, stews or stir-fries. Don't forget their versatile use in many Indian dishes as well.

HOW TO STORE Canned chickpeas will keep for several years. If you like to use dried chickpeas, store them in an airtight container for up to 8 months in a dark, dry location. Once cooked, chickpeas should be stored in the refrigerator and will keep for 4 days. I like to stock my cupboard with two cans of chickpeas I can reach for during the week.

Sometimes called garbanzo beans, chickpeas can be white or green but have a distinctive round, plump-looking shape and crunchy texture. Chickpeas are a delicious burst of health, full of complex carbohydrates, great protein, loads of fibre as well as B vitamins, iron and many more vitamins and essential minerals.

CURRY COCONUT CHICKPEAS

MAKES 2 CUPS (500 ML)

PLACE ALL THE INGREDIENTS into a saucepan over medium heat. Mix together until warm and serve as the perfect side dish to Macho Man Loaf (page 103). You can also add 1 cup (250 mL) of this prepared recipe overtop of Marathon Runner's Kale Salad (page 165) for an extra boost of energy. Store any leftovers in an airtight glass container in the refrigerator and consume within 3 days.

power food tip *Add ½ tsp (2 mL) cayenne pepper to increase the heat of this recipe if desired.*

1 can (14 oz/398 mL) chickpeas, rinsed and drained
2 tbsp (30 mL) coconut oil
1 tsp (5 mL) curry powder
Pinch Himalayan crystal salt
Pinch ground black pepper

HUNGRY HUNGRY HUMMUS

MAKES 4 CUPS (1 L)

RINSE THE CHICKPEAS and then place them into a food processor with all the remaining ingredients. Purée, adding more liquid as needed until the mixture reaches your desired consistency. Serve with some fresh sliced vegetables. Store your hummus in an airtight glass container in the refrigerator for 3 to 4 days.

~~~~~~~

power food tip Try boosting the nutritional value and flavour of your hummus by adding a variety of oils into the purée, such as 2 tbsp (30 mL) flax oil, sesame oil or hemp oil. You can even do a combo of all three oils. If the raw onion and garlic are too potent to your taste buds, you can first sauté them in 1 tsp (5 mL) olive oil and 1 tsp (5 mL) maple syrup over medium heat for 2 minutes.

2 cans (each 14 oz/398 mL) chickpeas

Juice of 2 lemons

1 large onion, diced

1 clove garlic, minced

2 tbsp (30 mL) oregano, chopped

3 tbsp (45 mL) tahini

1 tbsp (15 mL) prepared mustard

1 tsp (5 mL) honey

1 tsp (5 mL) Himalayan crystal salt

1 tsp (5 mL) ground black pepper

¼ cup (60 mL) hemp milk (page 81)

THE POWER OF LENTILS

WHY YOU SHOULD CARE There was a time not too long ago when I would fall asleep on the sofa not more then 30 minutes after finishing dinner. Sound familiar? What if I told you that lentils have the ability to control your blood sugar and leave you feeling satisfied and energized after your next meal? Would you try eating some? Here is the kicker: while you are sleeping on the sofa in your food coma, a lot of those calories you just ate are starting to be stored inside your fat cells, leading to weight gain. Give yourself the gift of lentils during dinner to ensure you have the power to walk up a flight of stairs while staying fit, trim and energized. Lentils can help you get up off the sofa!

HOW TO USE Lentils do not need to be soaked before using and do not require hours of cooking to be enjoyed. If using canned, just open and rinse. When using dried lentils, rinse 1 cup (250 mL) lentils and add 4 cups (1 L) water to a large saucepan. Bring to a boil, reduce heat and simmer uncovered until tender, about 30 minutes. Now your lentils are ready to use in so many great recipes.

Breakfast: Purée ½ cup (125 mL) cooked lentils and add 2 tsp (10 mL) each of hemp seeds, ground sesame seeds and ground flaxseeds to thicken the mixture into a paste. Spread over whole-grain toast with a little natural honey or applesauce and enjoy.

Lunch/Snack: Try stocking a can of lentils at work or in your school locker so you can add some to your soups or salads. Blending them into a dip is one way to give yourself a powerful helping of energy, sure to keep you going all day.

Dinner: Add cooked lentils into any vegetable recipe, such as burgers or a vegetable loaf. Try adding them into your stews, or purée a cup and turn it into a tasty, nutritious sauce.

HOW TO STORE Canned lentils will keep for several years. If you like to use dried lentils, store them in an airtight container for up to 8 months in a dark, dry location. Once cooked, lentils should be stored in the refrigerator and will keep for 4 days. Along with my chickpeas, I like to stock two cans in my cupboard for quick access throughout the week.

Lentils are a versatile Power Food when creating nutritious recipes in your kitchen. Like most legumes, you can expect loads of fibre, good-quality complex carbohydrates and a healthy dose of iron in every bite. Eating lentils any time of day will ensure you enjoy sustained energy when you need it.

SUN-DRIED TOMATO AND LENTIL SALAD

MAKES 2 LARGE SERVINGS

SOAK THE SUN-DRIED TOMATOES in a small bowl of water for 1 hour. When the tomatoes have soaked, chop them into small pieces. If using canned lentils, rinse with fresh water, drain and place them in a large salad bowl. Add the soaked tomatoes and the remaining ingredients (except the almonds) to the bowl containing the lentils and mix. Garnish with the crushed almonds overtop.

¼ cup (60 mL) sun-dried tomatoes

1 can (14 oz/398 mL) lentils

2 cups (500 mL) spinach

3 tbsp (45 mL) rosemary, chopped

½ tsp (2 mL) Himalayan crystal salt

¼ cup (60 mL) almonds, crushed, for garnish

~~~~~~~~

power food tip *Try any one of my tasty dressing recipes to finish off this salad with style, such as Heart-Warming Thai Dressing (page 147) or Classic Ginger Dressing (page 172).*

LENTIL SHEPHERD'S PIE

IN A LARGE SAUCEPAN, cook the diced potatoes in boiling water until tender, about 15 minutes. Drain the potatoes, then place them into a food processor with the hemp milk and coconut oil and blend. Remove your now mashed potatoes from the food processor and set aside.

Preheat the oven to 350°F (180°C). Next, in a small frying pan, sauté the onion and garlic in a little olive oil for 2 minutes. In your cleaned food processor, combine the sautéed onion and garlic and the remaining ingredients, except the mashed potatoes. Blend the ingredients together lightly to ensure the mixture remains chunky. Place the mixture into a deep 12-inch (30 cm) pie dish. (Alternatively, you could use an 8-inch/20 cm square glass baking dish or rectangular dish of equivalent size.) Spread the mashed potatoes overtop and bake in the preheated oven for 30 minutes. Store any leftovers in an airtight glass container in the refrigerator and eat within 3 to 4 days.

6 medium potatoes, diced

½ cup (125 mL) hemp milk (page 81)

2 tbsp (30 mL) coconut oil

1 medium onion, diced

4 cloves garlic, minced

2 cans (each 14 oz/398 mL) lentils

1 egg

1 cup (250 mL) carrots, chopped

1 cup (250 mL) broccoli, chopped

2 tbsp (30 mL) basil, chopped

2 tbsp (30 mL) rosemary, chopped

1 tbsp (15 mL) prepared mustard

1 tsp (5 mL) Himalayan crystal salt

1 tsp (5 mL) ground black pepper

power food tip *Garnish with a healthy serving of ground nuts or seeds overtop of each cooked piece to increase the flavour and nutritional value of every bite.*

HEART-HEALTHY LENTIL SOUP

MAKES 4 SERVINGS

PLACE ALL THE INGREDIENTS into a medium saucepan over high heat and bring to a boil. Reduce heat and simmer covered for 30 minutes. A large steaming bowl of this soup is perfect on a cold day to help warm your bones. Garnish your bowl with the hemp seeds or chopped almonds, if using. This soup would be great to freeze in an airtight glass container for up to 3 months. Just be sure to cool it down before freezing to avoid breaking your glass container.

~~~~~~~~~

power food tip *Use a hand blender to purée your soup to give it a smoother texture. The smoother it is, the easier it is to digest, which provides your body with more available energy.*

1 can (14 oz/398 mL) lentils

3 cups (750 mL) water

1 onion, diced

4 cloves garlic, diced

¼ cup (60 mL) rosemary, chopped

½ tsp (2 mL) Himalayan crystal salt

½ tsp (2 mL) ground black pepper

1 tbsp (15 mL) hemp seeds or chopped
   almonds for garnish (optional)

THE POWER OF BLACK BEANS

WHY YOU SHOULD CARE There are certain times throughout the year when many of us know we are going to overeat. Thanksgiving and Christmas are two perfect examples. At times like these we often ignore our body's "full" signal while we reach for a second dessert, right? This year during the holidays, be sure to include black beans on the menu. No, black beans do not make it okay to overeat, but they do have the power, thanks to their amazing combination of fibre and protein, to help move food through your stomach into your colon at a healthier pace. This means you will spend less energy on digestion and more energy on walking back to the buffet line for more—or not.

HOW TO USE If you are using canned black beans, rinse them off with fresh water before eating to remove much of the added salt and oils. Soak dried black beans for 4 to 6 hours before cooking, which helps reduce the cooking time. Once they have soaked, drain the beans and rinse them well. Place them into a saucepan, cover them with water and bring to a boil. Reduce heat and simmer uncovered until the beans are soft all the way through, about 45 minutes. Once cooked, drain, rinse and store in the refrigerator.

Breakfast: Blend some black beans with a little maple syrup and enjoy a morning burst of sustained energy. You can even spread this as a topping on your toast.

Lunch/Snack: Add a handful of black beans to your soup, or toss some into your salad. Throw a handful into a wrap or sandwich.

Dinner: Black beans are a great thickener for gravies, soups and stews and provide a hearty texture as a meat replacement in many of my recipes. Try them crushed up in a sauce or as a base for veggie burgers.

HOW TO STORE Canned black beans will keep for several years. If you like to use dried black beans, store them in an airtight container for up to 8 months in a dark, dry location. Once cooked, black beans should be stored in the refrigerator and will keep for 4 days. Stock two cans in your kitchen cupboard or pantry for quick access throughout the week.

> *Black beans, so easily recognizable because of their colour, are held in high regard for their health benefits all over the world. This is because they are low in fat and contain valuable minerals such as iron, calcium, potassium and magnesium and B vitamins. Black beans also contain an almost magical combination of fibre and protein to keep you fit and strong.*

BLACK BEAN BRUSCHETTA

MAKES 6 CUPS (1.5 L)

IN A LARGE MIXING BOWL, mash the black beans with the hemp seeds and oil. Next place all the remaining ingredients into the bowl and gently mix together. Serve over Hemptastic Crackers (page 79).

~~~~~~~~

power food tip *Add 1 chopped avocado to the ingredients to make a fantastic guacamole dip to enjoy with your favourite chips or crackers.*

½ cup (125 mL) black beans, drained and rinsed
¼ cup (60 mL) hemp seeds
2 tbsp (30 mL) extra virgin olive oil
Juice of 1 lemon
4 tomatoes, diced
1 onion, diced
2 cloves garlic, minced
¼ cup (60 mL) basil, chopped
½ tsp (2 mL) Himalayan crystal salt
Pinch ground black pepper

HEART-HEALTHY GRAVY

MAKES 1 CUP (250 ML)

PLACE ALL THE INGREDIENTS into a food processor and blend together. Add more water as needed until the gravy reaches your desired consistency. There is no need to heat this recipe, but feel free to do so if you want your gravy warmed.

~~~~~~~~

power food tip *Pour this gravy over Sweet Potato and Turnip Mash or Yummy Yam Fries (both on page 187) and enjoy without any feelings of guilt.*

1 can (14 oz/398 mL) black beans, drained and rinsed
2 tsp (10 mL) soy sauce
1 tsp (5 ml) prepared mustard
2 cloves garlic, minced
½ tsp (2 mL) Himalayan crystal salt
1 tsp (5 mL) ground black pepper
¼ cup (60 mL) water

CORN AND BLACK BEAN SALAD

MAKES 3 CUPS (750 ML)

DRAIN THE BLACK BEANS and corn, and rinse with fresh water. Place the drained beans and corn and the remaining ingredients into a large salad bowl, gently mix together and serve.

~~~~~~~~

power food tip *To spice up this salad a bit, you can add 1 tsp (5 mL) cayenne pepper. A little bit of heat goes very well with this salad.*

1 can (14 oz/398 mL) black beans

1 can (14 oz/398 mL) corn

1 cup (250 mL) cherry tomatoes, diced

¼ cup (60 mL) cilantro, chopped

¼ cup (60 mL) lemon juice

¼ cup (60 mL) extra virgin olive oil

½ small onion, diced

1 tbsp (15 mL) balsamic vinegar

½ tsp (2 mL) Himalayan crystal salt

½ tsp (2 mL) ground black pepper

ULTIMATE VEGGIE **BURGERS**

MAKES 8 PATTIES

PREHEAT THE OVEN TO 350°F (180°C). Toast the bread and place it into a food processor. Process to make breadcrumbs. (You may wish to make extra breadcrumbs at this stage, for use later in the recipe.) Remove breadcrumbs from food processor and set aside. In a small frying pan, sauté the onion and garlic in the olive oil for 2 minutes. In a large mixing bowl, place the sautéed onions and garlic and the remaining ingredients, except the breadcrumbs. Place the mixture into the food processor and blend. Return this mixture to your large mixing bowl and mix in the breadcrumbs. Using your hands, form the mixture into 8 to 10 patties. If your mixture is too moist, try adding another cup of toasted breadcrumbs. Place on a baking sheet and bake in the preheated oven for 35 minutes. Alternatively, you could barbecue the burgers if you prefer.

〜〜〜〜〜〜

power food tip *Serve each patty inside some Swiss chard to replace a bun as a great way to enjoy a fresh burger experience.*

5 slices sprouted grain bread

1 medium onion, diced

4 cloves garlic, minced

2 tbsp (30 mL) extra virgin olive oil

2 cans (each 14 oz/398 mL) black beans, drained and rinsed

1 egg

2 tsp (10 mL) lemon juice

2 cups (500 mL) chopped vegetables of your choice

1 tbsp (15 mL) prepared mustard

2 tbsp (30 mL) your favourite spices

2 tbsp (30 mL) your favourite herbs

1 tsp (5 mL) Himalayan crystal salt

1 tsp (5 mL) ground black pepper

THE POWER OF GREEN PEAS

WHY YOU SHOULD CARE Sitting in traffic for three hours a day while travelling to and from work left me dazed and confused from all the car exhaust fumes I would inhale. To make it worse, I was a smoker back in the day. I didn't know it at the time, but the number of free radicals attacking my cells was no doubt astronomical, and I felt it. I was tired all the time, was not sleeping well and was overweight. Controlling the impact free radicals have on your healthy cells during your daily routine is key to slowing the aging process and living an energized life. Green peas are a special Power Food in that they contain a large amount of vitamin C, which acts as an antioxidant to help fight off those nasty free radicals. So the next time you find yourself sitting in traffic or inhaling cigarette smoke, be sure to eat some fresh green peas to enjoy the extra antioxidant protection.

HOW TO USE Dried split green peas do not need to be soaked before using and do not require hours of cooking. If using canned peas, just drain and rinse. If using dried peas, rinse 1 cup (250 mL) and add 4 cups (1 L) water to a saucepan. Bring to boil, reduce heat and simmer uncovered until tender, about 30 minutes. Your peas are now ready to use in many great recipes.

Breakfast: Blend together ½ cup (125 mL) cooked split green peas with 2 tbsp (30 mL) each of hemp seeds, ground sesame seeds and ground flaxseeds. Add 1 tsp (5 mL) maple syrup if you prefer a sweet mix. Spread this mixture over whole-grain toast for a very powerful start to your day.

Lunch/Snack: I love snacking on fresh green peas when in season. I also enjoy taking a little split pea soup to work for an energizing lunch.

Dinner: Add fresh or cooked green peas into your pasta, or use them in your next batch of vegetable burgers. They also taste great mixed in with quinoa or brown rice and topped with crushed almonds as a healthy dinner option.

HOW TO STORE Fresh green peas will keep up to 7 days in the refrigerator. Canned green peas will keep for several years. Frozen green peas are also a great addition to a healthy diet, as most vegetables are flash frozen at the time of packaging, which preserves much of their nutritional value. If you like to use dried green peas, store them in an airtight container for up to 8 months in a dark, dry location. Once cooked, green peas should be stored in the refrigerator and will keep for 4 days. Why not stock a couple of cans for quick access throughout the week?

You may not think of green peas as a Power Food, but that is exactly what they are. Their sweet taste makes them a great addition to many recipes, and adding them will boost your intake of vitamin C. This vitamin along with great fibre, vitamin K, loads of B vitamins and protein are what make green peas—those symmetrical pearls of the legume world—so powerful.

GOING-FOR-GOLD GREEN PEA DIP

MAKES 3 CUPS (750 ML)

SOAK THE ALMONDS for 12 hours in 2 cups (500 mL) water. Drain and rinse, and place into a food processor. Blend for 5 seconds. Add the remaining ingredients and blend until the mixture reaches your desired consistency. I like mine a bit chunky, but smooth is also very good. If your dip is too thick, you could add 1 tbsp (15 mL) hemp milk (page 81) or the same amount of water. I love serving this dip with my Hemptastic Crackers (page 79) or Sweet Potato and Turnip Mash (page 187). Store any leftovers in an airtight glass container in the refrigerator and consume within 4 days.

½ cup (125 mL) almonds

1 can (14 oz/398 mL) green peas, drained and rinsed

¼ cup (60 mL) water

2 tsp (10 mL) lime juice

¼ cup (60 mL) cilantro, diced

1 tsp (5 mL) grated ginger

½ tsp (2 mL) Himalayan crystal salt

½ tsp (2 mL) ground black pepper

power food tip   I prefer my dip to have a bit of heat. If you do as well, feel free to add ½ tsp (2 mL) cayenne pepper to this recipe.

A SIDE OF CREAMY GREEN PEAS

MAKES 2 SERVINGS

IN A MEDIUM SAUCEPAN over low heat, melt the coconut oil with the hemp milk and salt. Add the remaining ingredients and stir until the mixture is warm. This is a great side dish to take to a potluck party or serve with Ultimate Veggie Burgers (page 73). Store any leftovers in an airtight glass container in the refrigerator and consume within 4 days.

2 tbsp (30 mL) coconut oil

1 tbsp (15 mL) hemp milk (page 81)

½ tsp (2 mL) Himalayan crystal salt

1 can (14 oz/398 mL) green peas, drained and rinsed

1 tbsp (15 ml) parsley, chopped

1 tbsp (15 mL) chia seeds

½ tsp (2 mL) ground black pepper

power food tip   Once they are warm, you can place your creamy green peas into a food processor and blend to make another fantastic healthy dip for vegetables or crackers.

SPLIT PEA SOUP

MAKES 6 SERVINGS

BRING THE WATER to a boil in a large saucepan and add all the other ingredients. Reduce heat and simmer covered over low heat for 30 minutes. Purée the soup with a hand blender until it reaches your desired consistency. Freeze any leftover soup to eat another day.

~~~~~~~~

power food tip *Increase the nutritional value of this hearty soup by adding either quinoa or ground nuts of your choice to each bowl.*

5 cups (1.25 L) water
2½ cups (625 mL) split green peas
6 large carrots, diced
3 celery stalks, diced
1 large onion, diced
4 cloves garlic, minced
¼ cup (60 mL) grated ginger
½ tsp (2 mL) Himalayan crystal salt
½ tsp (2 mL) ground black pepper

BEETS
BLACK GINGER ALMONDS
BEANS amaranth
vegetables
chickpeas GARLIC BROWN
seeds fruits RICE
GOJI BLUEBERRIES PECANS PISTACHIOS GREEN PEAS
BERRIES grains AVOCADOS nuts
WHOLE OATS CASHEWS
QUINOA KALE LENTILS
COCONUT
legumes

THE POWER OF COCONUT

WHY YOU SHOULD CARE More than a few people close to me suffer from dry skin, dandruff, eczema or psoriasis. Perhaps you also know someone who is tired of feeling the constant burn, annoying itch and unpleasant look and feel of these conditions. The good news is that some Power Foods can help alleviate or eliminate these symptoms for life. Coconut is one such food that can help. By eating 2 tbsp (30 mL) every day and rubbing 1 tsp (5 mL) into your skin where you need it, the healthy dose of unrefined antioxidants in coconut oil will feed your skin, bring relief and allow repair. Next time you reach for that expensive bottle of skin cream or shampoo, look in your cupboard and give some extra virgin coconut oil a try.

HOW TO USE Coconut can be found as oil, as butter, as milk and in its whole state as well as shredded, flaked or as a flour. Coconut oil is safe to use for sautéing vegetables and adds a welcome change in flavour to your stir-fries. The ideal way to consume coconut is straight from the source, if you are fortunate enough to live in a tropical climate. Otherwise, look for organic coconut products and enjoy coconut in all its multiple forms.

Breakfast: Sprinkle 2 tbsp (30 mL) shredded coconut into your cereal, smoothie, oatmeal or baked goods such as muffins or breads. Make your next smoothie with coconut milk, or smear some coconut oil on a piece of toast instead of butter.

Lunch/Snack: Try a little coconut oil in your salad dressings or soups. Spread a little coconut butter into a sandwich or wrap.

Dinner: Coconut milk is ideal in many recipes, such as curries and coconut soups, or added to a dip for an energizing burst.

HOW TO STORE Coconut as oil, as butter, shredded or flaked will keep in your cupboard away from any heat source for 3 months. Canned coconut milk will keep for several months or years, depending on the date it was canned. Once opened, it should be refrigerated and used within 3 days. If you are buying fresh coconuts, store them in the refrigerator and eat them within 4 days.

> *Though its name suggests it is a nut, I've always regarded coconut as a fruit. In actual fact, this hairy, hard-shelled member of the palm family with the surprising white interior is a seed. When the coconut is young, it has properties like those of a fruit, and as it matures, it becomes nuttier. Coconut contains fibre, iron and protein and is one of the only sources of saturated fat that is healthy for you to consume.*

COCONUT SHAKALICIOUS

MAKES 4 CUPS (1 L)

SOAK THE DATES in ½ cup (125 mL) water for 30 minutes. After the dates have soaked, place all the ingredients, including the soaked dates and the date water, into a blender and blend until smooth.

~~~~~~~

power food tip *Add 1 avocado into the mix to increase your essential fatty acid intake as well as to thicken your smoothie.*

4 pitted dates, chopped

1 banana

3 tbsp (45 mL) cacao powder

1 tbsp (15 mL) almond butter

¼ cup (60 mL) almonds

¼ cup (60 mL) cashews

2 tbsp (30 mL) hemp seeds

1 cup (250 mL) coconut milk

1 cup (250 mL) water

TROPICAL SALSA

MAKES 8 CUPS (2 L)

PLACE ALL THE INGREDIENTS into a large mixing bowl and gently mix together. Serve with a fresh batch of You've Gone Crackers (page 181) or your chip of choice.

～～～～～

power food tip I often eat 2 cups (500 mL) of this salsa as an early dinner to nourish my body and avoid overloading my digestive system before bed: a great idea for keeping your immune system powered up.

½ cup (125 mL) shredded coconut

1 peach, peeled, pitted and diced

2 apricots, peeled, pitted and diced

2 avocados, peeled, pitted and chopped

1 red pepper, seeded and diced

3 tomatoes, diced

1 onion, chopped

1 cup (250 mL) parsley, chopped

1 cup (250 mL) cilantro, chopped

¼ cup (60 mL) mint, chopped

Juice of 1 orange

Juice of 1 lemon

Zest of ½ lemon

2 cloves garlic, minced

1 tbsp (15 mL) grated ginger

1 cup (250 mL) hemp seeds

½ tsp (2 mL) Himalayan crystal salt

½ tsp (2 mL) ground black pepper

MANGO DESSERT WHIP

MAKES 4 CUPS (1 L)

PLACE ALL THE INGREDIENTS into a blender and blend until smooth. Add more water as needed until the mixture reaches your desired consistency. This is great as a topping served over fresh seasonal fruit for a healthy dessert. Store in the refrigerator for 3 to 4 days.

～～～～～

power food tip I often eat this over my Optimal Athlete's Granola (page 82) about an hour before I head out for a mountain bike ride, a day of rock climbing or a ski trip in the backcountry.

2 mangos, peeled, pitted and diced

1 cup (250 mL) macadamia nuts or cashews

1 cup (250 mL) hemp seeds

1 tbsp (15 mL) coconut oil

1 tbsp (15 mL) pure vanilla extract

½ tsp (2 mL) cinnamon

1 cup (250 mL) water

MAGIC MACAROONS

MAKES 14 MACAROONS

PREHEAT THE OVEN to 350°F (180°C). Line a large baking sheet with waxed paper or parchment paper. In a large mixing bowl, mix together all the ingredients. Using your fingers, form the mixture into small teaspoon-size balls and place them onto the prepared baking sheet. Bake in the preheated oven for 15 minutes, or until golden brown. So easy and yummy!

≈≈≈

power food tip *Try adding ¼ cup (60 mL) cacao powder to make chocolate macaroons.*

3 cups (750 mL) shredded coconut

½ cup (125 mL) coconut sugar

4 egg whites

½ tsp (2 mL) pure vanilla extract

½ tsp (2 mL) cinnamon

¼ tsp (1 mL) Himalayan crystal salt

THE POWER OF GOJI BERRIES

WHY YOU SHOULD CARE Recently one of my clients emailed me asking what she could feed her five-year-old boy to help his immune system stay strong. He had been getting colds on and off every few months for years. His parents were frustrated and worried for him. Thanks to our own young daughter, Juliette, and to many of my clients, I have been spending lots of my time researching the ideal foods for boosting the power of our immune system. In all this research, goji berries keep showing up high on that list, because each little berry offers a powerful dose of polysaccharides. These long-chain sugars are world-renowned for their ability to feed your immune system and keep it strong and energized. Juliette loves goji berries, and many of my clients say their children also enjoy the taste and texture. Go ahead and give them a try. Next time you or your child has a cold, eat a handful of goji berries throughout the day for 3 to 4 days. We now eat them daily in our family and find they help keep our energy high and immune systems strong.

HOW TO USE Goji berries are usually found in their dried form. Think of dried raisins, but red. I enjoy eating them dried as a snack all day long to sustain my energy. I also soak them in water to plump them up and add them to salads, soups and many other Power of Food recipes. Juliette loves them after they have been soaked, when they are easier for smaller children to eat. I also grind a handful in my coffee grinder and turn them into the world's healthiest sugar or sweetener substitute. If you are fortunate to find goji berries in the wild or to grow them yourself, they are extra powerful picked right from the source.

Breakfast: Add goji berries into your smoothies, cold cereal and oatmeal or place them on top of your pancakes. You can even sprinkle a little ground goji berries into your coffee for an extra boost of power.

Lunch/Snack: Soaked goji berries make a fine addition to salads or soups. You can even blend some after soaking and make a great spread for your next sandwich or wrap. Mix your blended goji berries with some almond butter or tahini and power up your lunch in a big way. When in doubt, just eat them as a snack and enjoy the sustained energy.

Dinner: You will not go wrong by adding goji berries to your stir-fries. Try some as the best pizza topping ever, with some rice or in your next stew. Just add them, add them, add them for a more powerful immune system.

HOW TO STORE Dried goji berries will keep for several months in an airtight glass container in the cupboard away from any heat source. If ground, place your goji berries in an airtight glass jar and store them in the refrigerator for up to 1 week. If picked fresh, they will keep for 4 to 7 days in the refrigerator, but for maximum health benefits I would eat fresh goji berries right away.

Goji, goji, goji. Goji berries have become one of my top three Power Foods in the past few years. Not only are these bright-red, smooth-skinned, elongated berries (also called wolfberries) a complete protein, but they also contain excellent fibre, loads of antioxidants and 21 or more trace minerals, including iron and calcium. Their sweet taste makes them a great addition to any child's meal as an easy way to strengthen their immune system.

SWEET GOJI DRESSING

MAKES 1 CUP (250 ML)

SOAK THE GOJI BERRIES for 20 minutes in ½ cup (125 mL) water. Put the berries, soaking water and all the rest of the ingredients into a blender or food processor, and blend on high until well combined. Store any leftovers in an airtight glass jar in the refrigerator for up to 4 days.

~~~~~

power food tip *Add 2 tsp (10 mL) grated ginger to give a little heat to this fresh and vibrant dressing.*

¼ cup (60 mL) dried goji berries

Juice of ½ lime

Juice of ½ lemon

Juice of 1 orange

½ cup (125 mL) fresh basil, chopped

1 tbsp (15 mL) honey

½ tsp (2 mL) Himalayan crystal salt

1 tsp (2 mL) tahini

GOJI-COCONUT STRAWBERRY SORBET

MAKES 4 CUPS (1 L)

PLACE ALL THE INGREDIENTS into a blender and blend until smooth. Enjoy this sorbet right away or store in the refrigerator in an airtight glass container for 3 to 4 days. This is a great healthy treat to help satiate your sugar cravings.

~~~~~

power food tip *Add 1 tbsp (15 mL) cacao powder to the blender and enjoy a chocolate strawberry sorbet. You can also use different fruits to create a number of variations.*

½ cup (125 mL) dried goji berries

2 tbsp (30 mL) coconut oil

1 cup (250 mL) ice

1 cup (250 mL) frozen strawberries

1 cup (250 mL) Brazil nuts, soaked

2 tbsp (30 mL) honey

½ cup (125 mL) water

GUILT-FREE CHOCOLATE BARS

MAKES 8 TO 10 BARS

PLACE THE CACAO BUTTER into a bowl and put it into a dehydrator to melt. Alternatively, you can use your oven set at the lowest temperature. Line an 8-inch (20 cm) square baking dish with parchment paper.

While the cacao butter is melting, place all the remaining ingredients into a large bowl and mix. Add the melted cacao butter when it is ready. Mix well together and place into the prepared baking dish. The mixture will begin to harden within a matter of seconds, so work quickly.

Place the baking dish into the refrigerator for 1 hour to let set. Once hardened, cut the chocolate into 8 bars (or more, smaller bars, if you wish). Store in the freezer to enjoy as desired. These chocolate bars make fantastic energy snacks on your next hiking trip or when cross-country skiing or snowshoeing.

～～～～～～

power food tip · Spread the mixture into ice cube trays to create individual portions for quick on-the-go snacking. So good!

1 lb (500 g) raw cacao butter

1 cup (250 mL) cacao nibs

½ cup (125 mL) dried goji berries

½ cup (125 mL) dried cranberries or cherries

1 cup (250 mL) almonds, roasted and crushed

½ cup (125 mL) hemp seeds

¼ cup (60 mL) cacao powder

THE POWER OF AVOCADOS

WHY YOU SHOULD CARE If you are anything like me, you may have spent years of your life worrying about your weight. So many of the diets I tried when I was 40 pounds heavier focused on the number of calories I ate, and especially the fat content. This was a big reason I avoided eating avocados, until I did my own research and realized I had it all wrong. Yes, as much as 85% of an avocado is fat, but this is healthy fat that actually promotes weight loss.

The types of essential fatty acids found in avocado have been proven to act as anti-inflammatories. We all live with inflammation in our bodies, but how we manage this inflammation determines whether we will prevent, reverse or attract unwanted disease. When you live with inflammation, a lot of your energy is going to help keep your immune system powered up. This diversion of energy often compromises your digestive system. Without proper digestion, the inflammation cycle continues and weight gain can be a common side effect. The next time you look at an avocado in the grocery store and pass it by, think again and give it the love it deserves. It just may help you shed those final 10 pounds.

HOW TO USE Avocados' silky texture and creamy taste make for a delicious snack right out of their skin. I also mash them up, dice them into recipes or drop them into soups and smoothies as a healthy thickener and a great alternative to dairy.

Breakfast: Mash one up, mix in ½ tsp (2 mL) maple syrup and spread over toast. Alternatively, add half an avocado to your smoothie.

Lunch/Snack: Dice an avocado into your salad or mix it into your next soup. Enjoy an avocado as an afternoon snack for sustained energy. Turn one into a dip or spread to enjoy inside a sandwich or wrap.

Dinner: Avocados are great added to stews, made into guacamole or used as a pizza topping. They also work well as a thickener in pasta sauces, to give a creamy texture without the cream.

HOW TO STORE The freshness of an avocado all depends on when you get it in your hands. A ripe avocado is slightly soft to the touch. If it is too brown and mushy, your avocado has seen its last day. If it is too hard, place it by a window and let it ripen until a bit softer. Once open, refrigerate any remaining avocado in an airtight container with a little lemon juice coating any green parts, to ensure it does not go brown and stays fresher.

Avocados are one Power Food I have learned to love over the years. I did not grow up eating them, but now I can't live without these dark-skinned, pear-shaped wonders. After I became more familiar with avocados' high amount of healthy fat, I wanted to make them part of my family's diet. Avocados are also rich in B vitamins, fibre and vitamin C, making them one very powerful food.

GO-TIME GUACAMOLE

MAKES 2 CUPS (500 ML)

USING A FORK, mash the avocados in a large bowl with the lemon
and lime juices as well as the salt and pepper. Be sure to leave the
avocado a little chunky, unless you prefer your guacamole to be
smooth. Now add the rest of the ingredients and mix together. I love
eating this guacamole on top of my Ultimate Veggie Burgers (page 73).
Store any leftovers in an airtight glass container in the refrigerator
for up to 4 days.

power food tip *Replace the olive oil with flax oil or hemp oil to increase
the quality of essential fatty acids you consume. This recipe is also delicious
with a few nuts or seeds added to create a different take on this guacamole.*

2 avocados, peeled, pitted and
   chopped
Juice of 1 lemon
Juice of 1 lime
½ tsp (2 mL) Himalayan crystal salt
½ tsp (2 mL) ground black pepper
½ red pepper, seeded and diced
4 cherry tomatoes, chopped
¼ cup (60 mL) extra virgin olive oil
½ onion, diced
3 cloves garlic, minced
½ cup (125 mL) cilantro, chopped

DREAMY AVOCADO DRESSING

MAKES 1 CUP (250 ML)

PLACE ALL THE INGREDIENTS into a blender and blend until smooth. Add more water as needed until the mixture reaches your desired consistency. Store any leftovers in an airtight jar in the refrigerator for up to 4 days.

~~~~~~

power food tip *This is a great dressing to take to work and eat with freshly cut seasonal vegetables as an energy-boosting snack.*

1 avocado, peeled, pitted and chopped

2 tbsp (30 mL) lime juice

3 tbsp (45 mL) flax oil, hemp oil or extra virgin olive oil

1 tsp (5 mL) prepared mustard

1 clove garlic, minced

1 tsp (5 mL) cumin

½ tsp (2 mL) Himalayan crystal salt

1 tsp (5 mL) ground black pepper

¼ cup (60 mL) water

HEART-WARMING THAI DRESSING

MAKES 2 CUPS (500 ML)

SOAK THE CHOPPED DATES for 20 minutes in 1 cup (250 mL) water. After the dates have soaked, place all the ingredients, including the soaked dates and the date water, into a blender and blend together. Add more water as needed until the mixture reaches your desired consistency. This dressing is perfect drizzled overtop of my Marathon Runner's Kale Salad (page 165). Store any leftovers in an airtight glass jar in the refrigerator for up to 4 days.

~~~~~~

power food tip *Add an extra avocado and ¼ cup (60 mL) chia seeds to the blender and enjoy this dressing as a dip with some fresh vegetables.*

¼ cup (60 mL) pitted dates, chopped

1 avocado, peeled, pitted and chopped

¼ cup (60 mL) cilantro, chopped

1 tsp (5 mL) cayenne pepper

1 tsp (5 mL) grated ginger

¼ tsp (1 mL) Himalayan crystal salt

1 cup (250 mL) water

SUMMER AVOCADO MANGO SALAD

MAKES 2 SERVINGS

PLACE THE SPINACH onto a large plate and place the pieces of fruit overtop. Drizzle the lime juice overtop and garnish with the chopped mint.

~~~~~~~~~

power food tip *Add 3 tbsp (45 mL) hemp seeds and enjoy this salad as a light dinner option.*

1 cup (250 mL) spinach

1 avocado, peeled, pitted and cut into bite-size pieces

1 mango, peeled, pitted and cut into bite-size pieces

½ cup (125 mL) fresh blueberries

1 grapefruit, peeled, pitted and cut into bite-size pieces

Juice of ½ lime

2 tbsp (30 mL) mint, chopped, for garnish

SPICY CHOCOLATE AVOCADO SALAD

MAKES 6 CUPS (1.5 L)

SOAK THE GOJI BERRIES in 1 cup (250 mL) water for 30 minutes. Meanwhile, in a small frying pan over medium heat, sauté the onion in the olive oil for 5 minutes. After the goji berries have soaked, drain them, discarding the water. Place the soaked berries into a large mixing bowl with the sautéed onions. Next add all the remaining ingredients and gently combine. This is a tasty side dish to accompany my Ultimate Veggie Burgers (page 73).

~~~~~~~~~

power food tip *Feel free to remove the seeds from the jalapeño if you want to reduce the heat of this salad.*

½ cup (125 mL) dried goji berries

½ onion, diced

2 tbsp (30 mL) extra virgin olive oil

2 avocados, peeled, pitted and diced

2 tomatoes, diced

¼ cup (60 mL) mint, chopped

1 tbsp (15 mL) cacao powder

½ jalapeño, minced

½ tsp (2 mL) Himalayan crystal salt

Juice of 1 lemon

CHILLED AVOCADO AND CILANTRO SOUP

MAKES 2 CUPS (500 ML)

PLACE ALL THE INGREDIENTS into a blender and blend until smooth. Alternatively, place all the ingredients in a saucepan with a flat bottom and blend using a hand blender. Add more water as needed until the soup reaches your desired consistency. This is a cold soup. If you prefer this soup warm, heat it in a saucepan over low heat while stirring continuously. This pairs perfectly with a slice of Rawtastic Pizza (page 182).

1 avocado, peeled, pitted and chopped

1 cup (250 mL) cilantro, chopped

2 tbsp (30 mL) lemon juice

½ tsp (2 mL) Himalayan crystal salt

1 cup (250 mL) water

≈≈≈≈≈

power food tip   Add a little cooked quinoa or a few hemp seeds or ground almonds to enhance the nutritional value of this tasty green soup.

THE POWER OF BLUEBERRIES

WHY YOU SHOULD CARE Most days while I am racing out the door to my next Power of Food event, I find myself reaching into my pockets to ensure I have my car keys. Usually I am forced to stop and try to remember where I left them before the moment turns into one of panic. I am thankful my memory is fuelled by living food, blueberries being one of the best. Memory loss is not an age-related symptom. It can happen to anyone at any time, as I am sure many of you can attest to. Thanks to their super-powerful antioxidant qualities, blueberries can help to prevent free radicals—molecules responsible for rapid aging and tissue damage—from attacking your cell structure. Eating a healthy dose of blueberries every day is the ideal way to ensure your memory stays sharp.

HOW TO USE Eat blueberries fresh and add them to smoothies, salads, cereal and oatmeal. Make them into a jam or spread. You can find blueberries dried, in a liquid form, as a jam or freeze-dried as a powder as well.

Breakfast: Try mashing a handful of blueberries with a fork and spreading them on top of some toast along with almond butter. Add a handful of berries to your morning smoothie or eat on top of your oatmeal or cereal. They add loads of flavour inside pancake batter and baked goods such as muffins, scones or breads.

Lunch/Snack: Add some berries to your salads for a refreshing twist, or munch on them as a healthy fresh snack. I like using dried blueberries in some of my trail mixes for a nice sweet kick.

Dinner: Blueberries will add a sweet tang when blended into many soup recipes. They also work well added to a wrap or stuffed along with quinoa into hollowed-out squash or red peppers.

HOW TO STORE Fresh blueberries should be kept in the refrigerator for up to 3 to 4 days. Dried blueberries will keep for several months in the cupboard in an airtight container, as will freeze-dried powdered blueberries. Blueberry juice should be consumed within 24 hours of being made.

> *Blueberries are a world-renowned "power fruit" native to North America. The next time you eat blueberries right from the bush, you will be, truly, eating locally. Super high in antioxidants, this full-flavoured, sweet-tasting indigo-coloured berry is rich in vitamin C and packs a little punch of fibre in every bite.*

WELCOME TO THE GUN SHOW SMOOTHIE

MAKES 6 CUPS (1.5 L)

PLACE ALL THE INGREDIENTS into a blender and blend until smooth. Add more water as necessary until the mixture reaches your desired consistency.

~~~~~~

power food tip *Substitute strawberries for the blueberries and Brazil nuts for the walnuts to try one of endless possible variations to this smoothie recipe.*

½ cup (125 mL) fresh blueberries

½ cup (125 mL) kale, chopped

1 banana

1 tsp (5 mL) maca powder

1 tsp (5 mL) cacao powder

1 tbsp (15 mL) coconut oil

1 tsp (5 mL) honey

½ cup (125 mL) walnuts

½ cup (125 mL) hemp seeds

4 cups (1 L) water

BLUEBERRY VINAIGRETTE

MAKES 1 CUP (250 mL)

PLACE ALL THE INGREDIENTS into a blender and blend until smooth. This dressing goes very well mixed in with Quinoa Greek Salad (page 113) or added to my Hungry Hungry Hummus recipe (page 120). Store any leftovers in an airtight glass jar in the refrigerator for up to 7 days.

~~~~~~

power food tip *Chop up 1 cup (250 mL) kale. Place the chopped kale in a bowl with ¼ cup (60 mL) of this dressing. Massage the dressing into your kale, and enjoy this as a refreshing salad topped with ¼ cup (60 mL) hemp seeds.*

½ cup (125 mL) fresh blueberries

½ cup (125 mL) extra virgin olive oil

3 tbsp (45 mL) balsamic vinaigrette

2 tbsp (30 mL) lemon juice

1 tbsp (15 mL) prepared mustard

½ tsp (2 mL) Himalayan crystal salt

½ tsp (2 mL) ground black pepper

CHOCOLATE BLUEBERRY PIE

MAKES ONE 9-INCH (23 CM) PIE

CRUST Place all the crust ingredients into a food processor and blend until the mixture has a batter-like consistency. Evenly spread the batter over the bottom of a deep 9-inch (23 cm) pie dish. Clean your food processor before you begin to make the pie filling.

FILLING Soak the chopped dates in 3 cups (750 mL) of water for 20 minutes. Drain. Place the dates, blueberries and remaining filling ingredients, except the garnish, into the food processor and blend together. Once blended, spread the filling over the prepared crust. Garnish with the dried blueberries, hemp seeds or roasted chopped almonds. This very decadent pie gets even better when served with a teaspoon of Strawberry Cashew Cream (page 71).

~~~~~~~~~~

power food tip *Try using another fruit, such as strawberries, to change up this delightful no-bake pie. You can make endless variations to wow your friends and family.*

CRUST

2 cups (500 mL) walnuts

1 cup (250 mL) chia seeds, ground

1 tsp (5 mL) cinnamon, ground

2 tbsp (30 mL) water

2 tbsp (30 mL) honey

FILLING

2 cups (500 mL) pitted dates, chopped

1 cup (250 mL) fresh blueberries

¼ cup (60 mL) water

2 tsp (10 mL) cacao powder

1 tsp (5 mL) cinnamon

½ tsp (2 mL) nutmeg

½ tsp (2 mL) allspice, ground

2 cups (500 mL) almonds, ground

1 cup (250 mL) hemp seeds

½ cup (125 mL) dried blueberries, hemp seeds or chopped roasted almonds for garnish

GET YOUR MOTOR STARTED DRINK

MAKES 4 CUPS (1 L)

PLACE ALL THE INGREDIENTS into a 4-cup (1 L) glass jar and shake together. This is what I drink first thing every morning to help get my digestion started.

~~~~~~~~~~

power food tip *Add 1 tsp (5 mL) natural powdered probiotics to this drink to help boost the power of your immune system.*

2 cups (500 mL) water

2 cups (500 mL) water, warm

Juice of ½ lemon

½ tsp (2 mL) Himalayan crystal salt

OUTRAGEOUS OLIVE TAPENADE

MAKES 1 CUP (250 ML)

PLACE ALL THE INGREDIENTS except the olive oil into a food processor and blend together. Add the olive oil a little at a time until the mixture reaches your desired consistency. This recipe is delicious served with You've Gone Crackers (page 181) or added as a topping to my Rawtastic Pizza (page 182). Store any leftovers in an airtight glass container in the refrigerator for up to 6 days.

~~~~~~~~~~

power food tip *Make extra because this recipe can be used as a quick snack before you race out the door.*

2 cloves garlic, minced

1 cup (250 mL) green olives, pitted and diced

1 cup (250 mL) black olives, pitted and diced

2 tbsp (30 mL) capers

1 tsp (5 mL) oregano, chopped

2 tsp (10 mL) rosemary, chopped

¼ cup (60 mL) parsley, chopped

2 tbsp (30 mL) lemon juice

2 tsp (10 mL) ground black pepper

3 tbsp (45 mL) extra virgin olive oil

ACTIVE KIDS BANANA CRÊPES

MAKES 4 CRÊPES

PLACE ALL THE INGREDIENTS into a blender and blend together until smooth. If the batter is too thick, add a little more hemp milk until it pours easily. Spread the batter evenly onto a dehydrator tray. Use 4 trays to be sure to evenly spread the batter to your desired crêpe thickness. The thicker the crêpe, the longer it takes to dehydrate or bake. Dehydrate at 115°F (46°C) for 6 hours, then flip over and dehydrate for another 6 hours. If using an oven, spread the batter onto a baking sheet lined with waxed paper or parchment paper, and bake at the lowest temperature for 30 minutes on one side and 30 minutes on the other. Bake for longer if you want your crêpes a little more cooked. You can reheat any leftover crêpes in your dehydrator or oven, but they taste delicious when cold. Store any leftovers in an airtight glass container in the refrigerator for up to 4 days.

2 bananas

2 cups (500 mL) cashews

1 cup (250 mL) hemp seeds

2 tbsp (30 mL) honey

2 tbsp (30 mL) pure vanilla extract

1 cup (250 mL) hemp milk (page 81)

~~~~~~

power food tip   *Fill each crêpe with some fresh seasonal berries and a healthy scoop of Strawberry Cashew Cream (page 71). Your kids will love these!*

PEAR DRESSING

MAKES 2 CUPS (500 ML)

PLACE ALL THE INGREDIENTS into a blender and blend until smooth. Add more water until the mixture reaches your desired consistency. Try adding ¼ cup (60 mL) of this dressing to 1 cup (250 mL) of Amaranth Tabbouleh (page 109) and serve overtop a bed of spinach. Store any leftovers in an airtight glass jar in the refrigerator for up to 3 days.

~~~~~~

power food tip *Omit the water from this recipe to make a great topping for pizza or a mixture to put between two pieces of your favourite bread as a lunchtime sandwich.*

1 pear, peeled, cored and chopped

½ cup (125 mL) artichoke hearts

¼ cup (60 mL) onion, chopped

1 clove garlic, minced

1 tsp (5 mL) grated ginger

Juice of 1 lemon

¼ cup (60 mL) parsley, chopped

½ cup (125 mL) hemp seeds

1 tsp (5 mL) Himalayan crystal salt

Pinch ground black pepper

1 cup (250 mL) water

PEACHY CREAM DRESSING

MAKES 2 CUPS (500 ML)

PLACE ALL THE INGREDIENTS into a blender and blend until smooth. Add more water as needed until the mixture reaches your desired consistency. Pour the dressing over mixed greens or use it with fresh vegetables as a tangy dip. Store any leftovers in an airtight glass jar in the refrigerator for 4 days.

~~~~~~

power food tip *Here's a bonus recipe for you using this dressing. Slice 1 large zucchini into thin pieces using a mandoline and marinate them in this dressing overnight. The next morning, place the zucchini slices on a dehydrator tray and dehydrate for 4 hours at 115°F (46°C). Alternatively, using an oven, place the slices on a baking sheet lined with waxed paper or parchment paper, and bake at 300°F (150°C) for 20 to 30 minutes to enjoy some crunchy zucchini chips. Stored in an airtight glass container in the cupboard, these chips will keep for up to 2 weeks.*

1 peach, peeled, cored and pitted

¼ cup (60 mL) hemp seeds

¼ cup (60 mL) sun-dried tomatoes, chopped

1 tbsp (15 mL) prepared mustard

1 tbsp (15 mL) tahini

½ tsp (2 mL) grated ginger

Juice of ½ lemon

½ tsp (2 mL) turmeric

½ tsp (2 mL) Himalayan crystal salt

½ tsp (2 mL) ground black pepper

1½ cups (375 mL) water

AWESOME DRIED MANGO

MAKES 2 CUPS (500 mL)

PEEL THE SKIN OFF the mango. Slice the mango into thin pieces and place them onto dehydrator trays. Dehydrate at 115°F (46°C) for 24 hours. If using an oven, lay the mango slices on a baking sheet and bake at the lowest temperature for 30 minutes, with the oven door slightly ajar. If still moist after 30 minutes, flip each piece over and bake until dry. Stored in an airtight glass container in the cupboard, this dried mango will keep for several weeks.

≈≈≈≈≈

power food tip *Take this yummy treat on the road for a sweet, healthy snack that will provide a quick boost of energy.*

1 large mango

ONLINE BONUS

Visit PowerofFood.com to watch a video on how to prepare this recipe.

NOW THAT'S A HOT CHOCOLATE

MAKES 4 CUPS (1 L)

PLACE ALL THE INGREDIENTS into a medium saucepan over medium heat. Stir constantly while the mixture is heating to avoid burning the hot chocolate. Once the cacao butter starts to melt, reduce heat and continue stirring until fully melted. Drinking this is a super way to warm your entire body on a cold day or when returning from winter activities.

≈≈≈≈≈

power food tip *This is a great coffee replacement drink, for natural raw chocolate stimulates your body.*

3 cups (750 mL) hemp milk (page 81)
1 tbsp (15 mL) cacao butter
2 tbsp (30 mL) cacao powder
Pinch chili powder
1 tsp (5 mL) cinnamon
3 tbsp (45 mL) maple syrup

I CAN'T BELIEVE IT'S **APPLE PIE**

MAKES ONE 9-INCH (23 CM) PIE

CRUST Place the pecans, almonds and dates into a food processor and blend together. Once it is blended, evenly spread the mixture into a deep 9-inch (23 cm) pie dish to serve as the crust. Clean your food processor before you begin to make the pie filling.

FILLING Place 1 apple and all the other filling ingredients, except the garnish, into a food processor and blend together. Place the filling into a bowl. Add the second diced apple and mix into the filling. Spread the filling over the prepared crust. Add more chopped apples as desired. Garnish with ½ cup (125 mL) chopped pecans. I highly recommend topping each piece before serving with 1 tbsp (15 mL) Ultimate Chocolate Mousse (page 71). Store any leftovers in an airtight glass container in the refrigerator for up to 4 days.

power food tip *Replace the apples with any other fruit and voilà: instant pie with endless variations.*

CRUST

½ cup (125 mL) pecans

½ cup (125 mL) almonds

½ cup (125 mL) pitted dates, chopped

FILLING

2 apples, chopped (more as desired)

½ tsp (2 mL) cinnamon

½ tsp (2 mL) nutmeg

½ tsp (2 mL) allspice

2 tsp (10 mL) lemon juice

½ cup (125 mL) chopped pecans for garnish

CRUSHING CRANBERRY SAUCE

MAKES 2 CUPS (500 ML)

SOAK THE CHOPPED DATES in the apple juice for 20 minutes. After the dates have soaked, place them into a blender along with the apple juice, orange juice, whole cranberries and spices. Blend until the mixture reaches a smooth texture, then add the pecans and dried cranberries and blend some more. Serve 1 tbsp (15 mL) overtop of Easy Grain Risotto (page 106) or stuffed inside a hollowed-out butternut squash with some wild rice. Store any leftovers in an airtight glass container in the refrigerator for up to 6 days.

~~~~~~

power food tip *Spread this sauce thinly onto your dehydrator tray and dehydrate at 115°F (46°C) for 6 hours to enjoy a delicious fruit roll-up. Alternatively, use an oven set at the lowest temperature. Line a large baking sheet with parchment paper or waxed paper. Spread sauce on the paper and bake until dry enough to roll, about 60 minutes.*

½ cup (125 mL) pitted dates, chopped

1 cup (250 mL) apple juice

1 cup (250 mL) orange juice

1 cup (250 mL) cranberries, whole

1 tsp (5 mL) cinnamon

½ tsp (2 mL) nutmeg

½ tsp (2 mL) allspice

1 cup (250 mL) pecans, chopped

1 cup (250 mL) dried cranberries

I'LL HAVE A LITTLE EXTRA PLUM SAUCE

MAKES 4 CUPS (1 L)

5 IN 5

PLACE ALL THE INGREDIENTS into a food processor and blend together until smooth. Use as a garnish over soups or salads, or eat a little on its own as a refreshing snack.

~~~~~~

power food tip *Add 2 to 3 tbsp (30 to 45 mL) water to turn this recipe into a fantastic dressing.*

2 plums, pitted and diced

1 red pepper, seeded and chopped

1 cup (250 mL) cashews

¼ cup (60 mL) hemp seeds

Pinch Himalayan crystal salt

RAW-RAW **BROWNIES**

MAKES 8 BROWNIES

$5_{IN}5$

PLACE ALL THE INGREDIENTS into a food processor and blend together. Line an 8-inch (20 cm) square baking dish with waxed paper or parchment paper. Spoon the mixture evenly into the prepared pan and press it down using a fork until firm. You want the mixture to be about 1 inch (2.5 cm) thick. Refrigerate the pan for 1 hour to let harden, or eat right away if you like your brownies a bit softer. The harder they are, the easier they will be to cut and store. Once hardened, cut into small brownie-size pieces and freeze them, to be eaten when you desire.

~~~~~~~

power food tip   *Alternatively, using your hands, roll the finished mixture into small balls half the size of a golf ball and set aside. On a large plate, place ½ cup (125 mL) hemp seeds, shredded coconut or cacao powder. Roll each ball around the plate until coated. You now have homemade truffles to impress the guests at your next party.*

2 cups (500 mL) pitted dates, chopped

2 tbsp (30 mL) water

½ cup (125 mL) almond butter

3 tbsp (45 mL) cacao powder

BEETS
BLACK GINGER
BEANS amaranth
ALMONDS
vegetables
chickpeas GARLIC
BLUEBERRIES
BROWN
PISTACHIOS
seeds *fruits* RICE
GOJI PECANS GREEN PEAS
AVOCADOS
nuts
BERRIES *grains*
WHOLE OATS CASHEWS
QUINOA KALE
COCONUT LENTILS
legumes

THE POWER OF KALE

WHY YOU SHOULD CARE   Out of affection, I like to call kale the "Queen of Green." This was not always the case, for I grew up eating mainly iceberg lettuce or romaine in salads. I barely knew anything else existed. I was so set in my ways that I never noticed kale in my grocery store until I became overweight, pre-diabetic, tired and sick all the time. Somehow I picked up a piece of kale when I was in my late twenties and decided to eat it. It was not the most pleasurable food to eat at first, but before I knew it, kale had become a regular part of my daily diet. Almost immediately I felt my energy improve. My digestion become more regular and I felt fewer hunger cravings. The positive health impact of kale continued, and to this day I add a handful to my daily smoothies and make fresh green juices for the entire family. The list of health benefits of kale is long and worthy of an entire book of its own. If you are stuck in a habitual pattern of eating only iceberg lettuce or romaine, give the "Queen of Green" a try to enjoy a mighty boost to your health.

HOW TO USE   Kale can be found fresh in most grocery stores all year round. Of late you can also find kale juice in specialty food stores and some mainstream grocery stores. I like to purée any extra kale from my garden and freeze it to add to soups or stews when I feel the sniffles or a cold coming on.

Breakfast: Add a handful to your morning smoothie. I know this may sound odd, but trust me on this one—just do it.

Lunch/Snack: Classic Kale Chips (page 164) are one of my all-time-favourite snacks. They are easy to make and taste great. I also enjoy making kale salads for lunch and adding fresh chopped kale to my soups. Inserting a few pieces into a wrap or sandwich is a good idea as well.

Dinner: Steamed kale with quinoa is a great combo. Kale is also delicious added to a stew or stir-fry.

HOW TO STORE   Fresh kale will keep for up to 7 days in the refrigerator. Just keep in mind it is alive. The longer it sits, the more nutrients it loses. Fresh kale juice should be consumed within 8 to 24 hours to take full advantage of its health benefits and flavour.

Kale, with its curly deep-green or purple leaves, is one of the healthiest vegetables you can possibly eat. With each bite you are nourishing your body and mind with a large amount of vitamin C, vitamin K and vitamin A as well as fibre, iron, calcium and protein. Now that is some nutrient richness.

DRINK TO YOUR HEALTH

MAKES 4 CUPS (1 L)

PLACE ALL THE INGREDIENTS into a blender and blend on high until smooth. If you wish to remove the fibre, strain the juice through a cheesecloth over a large mixing bowl. If you have a juicer, feel free to use it for this recipe. Drinking this is a great way to replenish your cell structure and feel extra powerful.

~~~~~~

power food tip *Add 1 tsp (5 mL) chopped jalapeño to enjoy a little heat with your juice.*

1 small beet, chopped

1 celery stalk, chopped

½ bunch kale, chopped

½ cucumber, diced

1 apple, cored and diced

1 grapefruit, peeled and chopped

1 lemon, chopped, with skin on

¼ cup (60 mL) parsley, chopped

1 tsp (5 mL) grated ginger

GREEN GODDESS GOODNESS ELIXIR

MAKES 4 CUPS (1 L)

PLACE ALL THE INGREDIENTS in a blender and blend until smooth. Add more water if needed to reach your desired consistency. Enjoy this refreshing beverage any time of day.

~~~~~~

power food tip *Add 1 cup (250 mL) crushed ice to the blender and serve this as the perfect cooling drink on a hot summer afternoon.*

¼ cup (60 mL) kale, chopped

½ cup (125 mL) spinach, chopped

2 pitted, dates chopped

1 banana, chopped

½ tsp (2 mL) Himalayan crystal salt

4 cups (1 L) water

STRONGER MUSCLES DIP

MAKES 6 CUPS (1.5 L)

PLACE ALL THE INGREDIENTS into a food processor and blend together. Add more water as needed until the mixture reaches your desired consistency. Serve this dip with your favourite chips or try it with You've Gone Crackers (page 181). Store your dip in an airtight glass container in the refrigerator and consume within 4 days.

~~~~~

power food tip *This is a great recipe to enjoy if you are experiencing sore joints or looking to recover after a tough workout. All the healthy oil will help reduce inflammation and allow you to recover more quickly.*

3 carrots, chopped

3 celery stalks, chopped

1 red pepper, seeded and chopped

1 beet, chopped

2 apples, cored and chopped

1 cup (250 mL) kale, chopped

1 cup (250 mL) parsley, chopped

1 cup (250 mL) dill, chopped

¼ cup (60 mL) hemp oil

¼ cup (60 mL) flax oil

1 tbsp (15 mL) tahini

¼ tsp (1 mL) cayenne pepper

½ tsp (2 mL) Himalayan crystal salt

Pinch ground black pepper

½ cup (125 mL) water

CLASSIC KALE CHIPS

MAKES 18 CHIPS OR 1 LARGE BAG

CHOP THE KALE into chip-size pieces. Place all the ingredients except the kale into a large bowl and mix. Next add the kale and mix until well coated. Place the kale pieces onto dehydrator trays and dehydrate at 115°F (46°C) for 12 hours. If using an oven, lay the kale pieces on a baking sheet and bake at the lowest temperature for 30 minutes. If the chips are still moist after 30 minutes, bake for longer. Stored in an airtight glass container in the cupboard, your chips will keep for 7 days.

~~~~~

power food tip *Double up this recipe to ensure you have plenty of chips on hand. The more you make, the easier you will find it to avoid buying commercial potato chips.*

1 bunch kale

¼ cup (60 mL) soy sauce

2 tbsp (30 mL) lemon juice

1 tbsp (15 mL) prepared mustard

1 tbsp (15 mL) grated ginger

1 tbsp (15 mL) ground black pepper

ONLINE BONUS

Visit PowerofFood.com to watch a video on how to prepare this recipe.

MARATHON RUNNER'S KALE SALAD

MAKES 2 SERVINGS

SOAK THE CRANBERRIES in ½ cup (125 mL) water for 30 minutes. Meanwhile, place the chopped kale and lemon juice into a large mixing bowl. Using your hands, massage the kale and lemon juice together. The acid from the juice will help to break down the kale and make it easier to digest. After the cranberries have finished soaking, discard the water and add the soaked cranberries to the kale. Next add all the remaining ingredients, except the garnish, and gently mix together. Add a little Classic Ginger Dressing (page 172) overtop and serve garnished with the sesame seeds.

power food tip *Whether you are already a marathon runner or looking to get started, this salad is a perfect way to boost your energy and get you pumped up for a great workout. Eat 2 cups (500 mL) 1 hour before your next workout and feel your superhuman powers come to life.*

¼ cup (60 mL) dried cranberries

1 bunch kale, chopped

Juice of 1 lemon

½ pear, chopped

½ apple, chopped

½ red pepper, seeded and chopped

1 carrot, chopped

2 tbsp (30 mL) sesame seeds
   for garnish

CRANBERRY KALE SALAD

MAKES 1 SERVING

CHOP THE KALE into small pieces. Place the kale in a large mixing bowl with the lemon juice. Using your hands, massage the lemon juice into the kale. Be sure to really massage the lemon juice into the kale for a few minutes. The acid from the lemon juice will help to break down the kale without using any heat, preserving its full nutritional value. Cover and refrigerate the bowl for 20 minutes. Sprinkle the cranberries overtop and serve with Heart-Warming Thai Dressing (page 147) or Classic Ginger Dressing (page 172).

1 bunch kale

¼ cup (60 mL) lemon juice

½ cup (125 mL) dried cranberries

power food tip *In the summertime, replace the dried cranberries with 1 cup (250 mL) of fresh local seasonal berries to enhance your intake of vital antioxidants and add loads of extra flavour.*

BROCCOLI KALE CREAM SOUP

MAKES 6 SERVINGS

IN A BLENDER, blend half of the chopped vegetables with the water. In a large saucepan, bring the blended mix to a quick boil, and then reduce heat to simmer. Add all the remaining ingredients except the kale to the saucepan and simmer covered over low heat for 30 minutes. Once the soup has cooked, add the remaining chopped kale and serve immediately. This soup will keep in the refrigerator for 3 to 4 days or in the freezer for 3 to 4 months.

1½ heads broccoli, chopped into bite-size pieces

1 bunch kale, chopped

4 celery stalks, chopped

2 onions, chopped

3 cups (750 mL) water

4 cloves garlic, minced

1 tbsp (15 mL) coconut oil

6 cups (1.5 L) hemp milk (page 81)

½ tsp (2 mL) Himalayan crystal salt

Pinch ground black pepper

power food tip *Serve each bowl of soup with some Hemptastic Crackers (page 79) for a full-spectrum nutritional boost. Oh, yeah!*

OH MY, KALE GOMAE

MAKES 2 SERVINGS

CHOP THE KALE into small pieces. In a vegetable steamer, steam the kale until tender, about 5 minutes. While the kale is steaming, in a small frying pan over low heat, toast the sesame seeds for 2 minutes and then set aside to use as your garnish. Do not overcook the seeds. Place the remaining ingredients into a small saucepan over medium heat. Using a fork or spoon, continually stir until warm, approximately 3 to 5 minutes. Place the steamed kale into a large mixing bowl. Next add the warmed sauce and gently mix together. Garnish with the toasted sesame seeds and serve. This recipe makes a great companion for Lentil Shepherd's Pie (page 124).

≈≈≈≈≈

power food tip *To make this recipe a little more sweet and savoury, add another 1 tbsp (15 mL) soy sauce as well as 1 tbsp (15 mL) coconut sugar as you heat the sauce.*

1 bunch kale

¼ cup (60 mL) sesame seeds

1½ cups (375 mL) water

2 tbsp (30 mL) almond butter

1 tbsp (15 ml) soy sauce

¼ cup (60 mL) raisins

BARBECUE KALE **RIBS**

MAKES 6 TO 8 RIBS

IN A BOWL, soak the raisins, goji berries and Brazil nuts, in enough water to just cover them, for 1 hour. After they have soaked, place the raisins, berries and nuts along with the water and all the other ingredients, except the kale, into a food processor and blend together.

Once blended, place the mixture into a large bowl. Separate the kale leaves, rinse and pat dry. Using a spatula, scrape the mixture onto the full-length kale leaves. Be sure to coat as much of the kale as possible. Once they are coated, place the "ribs" on a dehydrator tray and dehydrate at 115°F (46°C) for about 12 hours (or overnight). If using an oven, place the kale on a baking sheet lined with parchment paper or waxed paper and bake at the lowest temperature for 30 minutes. If the kale "ribs" are still moist after this time, flip them over and bake for 30 minutes more.

≈≈≈

power food tip *These Barbecue Kale Ribs are great for sharing while watching the Saturday-night hockey game or Sunday-afternoon football match.*

¼ cup (60 mL) raisins

¼ cup (60 mL) dried goji berries

¼ cup (60 mL) Brazil nuts

¼ cup (60 mL) sesame seeds

1 tsp (5 mL) caraway seeds, ground

½ tsp (2 mL) cayenne pepper

Pinch Himalayan crystal salt

Pinch freshly ground black pepper

1 bunch kale

THE POWER OF GINGER

WHY YOU SHOULD CARE I relied on medication for years to combat excessive heartburn. Every day after eating lunch or dinner I would get a strong burning sensation in my esophagus and need to take an antacid to help alleviate my symptoms. I continued to eat processed foods and use antacids for many years, but you know how the saying goes, "I wish I had known then what I know now." Recently a client asked me what I eat to help with heartburn and ease digestion. I think you know the answer. A little grated ginger in some tea after a meal is my preferred digestive aid, and as for heartburn, I haven't experienced it for years. If you find yourself feeling extra full after a meal or suffering from heartburn, take 1 tsp (5 mL) grated ginger with hot tea and let the magic of this natural digestive do the rest.

HOW TO USE Ginger can be found as a tea, in cookies, in ginger ale and as a powder, but the ideal way to consume ginger is in its natural state. I grate ginger daily and add it to many of the foods I eat.

Breakfast: Drinking a glass of warm water with lemon juice and grated ginger is a great way to start your digestion for the day. I also enjoy a bit of grated ginger in my smoothie to give it a little spice.

Lunch/Snack: Adding ginger to your soups and including it in your daily vegetable juice are two more ways to eat this powerful food.

Dinner: Grated ginger features in many of my recipes, including stews, soups, salad dressings, dips, sauces and many more. Any time you would like to add a little extra heat, think of ginger first.

HOW TO STORE How long fresh ginger will keep will depend on how fresh it was when you purchased it. When buying fresh ginger, make sure it is firm and free of mould. Stored in the vegetable crisper of your refrigerator, firm ginger will keep for 7 to 14 days.

Native to Southeast Asia, bulbous, light-brown ginger root is grown all around the world and is renowned for its culinary contributions. Although ginger is considered either a spice or an herb depending on your source of information, I wanted to highlight it as a Power Food due to its extremely important anti-inflammatory and digestive-aid properties as well as its punchy aromatic flavour, featured in many of my recipes.

KICK-IT-UP CARROT JUICE

MAKES 6 CUPS (1.5 L)

PLACE ALL THE INGREDIENTS into a blender and blend until smooth. This juice is a great way to start your day or perfect after a light afternoon run. Store any leftovers in an airtight glass jar in the refrigerator and drink it within 24 hours.

～～～～～

power food tip Add 1 chopped onion, 2 chopped celery stalks, 2 minced cloves of garlic and 2 cups (500 mL) chia seeds to create a delicious dip for vegetables.

4 carrots, chopped

2 apples, cored and chopped

½ cucumber, chopped

½ cup (125 mL) parsley, chopped

½ tsp (2 mL) grated ginger

Juice of ½ lemon

Pinch Himalayan crystal salt

4 cups (1 L) water

SUPER VEGGIE QUINOA CRACKERS

MAKES ONE 9-INCH (23 CM) SQUARE CRACKER

PLACE ALL THE INGREDIENTS into a food processor and blend until smooth. Once blended, spread the mixture evenly ½ inch (1 cm) thick on a dehydrator tray. Dehydrate at 115°F (46°C) for 6 hours, then flip over the cracker and dehydrate for another 6 hours. If using an oven, spread the mixture onto a baking sheet and bake at the lowest temperature for 1 hour. If still moist after 1 hour of baking, flip over the cracker and bake until it reaches your desired crispness. Once done, break your cracker into bite-size pieces to enjoy as desired. Stored in an airtight glass container in the cupboard, these crackers will keep for 7 to 10 days.

～～～～～

power food tip Once you spread the mixture evenly on the dehydrator tray or baking sheet, use a knife to score lines where you would like to break the crackers apart once they are cooked.

2 cups (500 mL) quinoa, cooked

½ cup (125 mL) diced red pepper

½ cucumber, diced

¼ cup (60 mL) green onion, diced

½ cup (125 mL) basil, chopped

Juice of 1 lemon

¼ cup (60 mL) flaxseeds, ground

1 tsp (5 mL) grated ginger

2 tbsp (30 mL) curry powder

½ tsp (2 mL) Himalayan crystal salt

CLASSIC GINGER DRESSING

MAKES 1 CUP (250 ML)

PLACE ALL THE INGREDIENTS into a blender and blend until well mixed. This dressing pairs well with my Spring Quinoa Salad (page 112) or Summer Avocado Mango Salad (page 148). Store any leftover dressing in an airtight glass jar in the refrigerator for up to 4 days.

~~~~~~~~~

power food tip *Add 1 cup (250 mL) all-natural almond butter and serve as a tasty dip for vegetables or spring rolls.*

¾ cup (185 mL) extra virgin olive oil

2 tbsp (30 mL) toasted sesame oil

Juice of 1 lime

2 tsp (10 mL) soy sauce

3 tbsp (45 mL) maple syrup

1 tsp (5 mL) grated ginger

APPLE-GINGER BUTTERNUT SQUASH SOUP

MAKES 8 CUPS (2 L)

STEAM THE CHOPPED SQUASH until soft, about 20 minutes. After the squash is soft, place it with the remaining ingredients into a blender and blend until smooth. Your soup should be a bit warm from the steamed squash, but if you want it hotter, heat it in a saucepan over low heat while stirring continuously. Store any leftovers in an airtight glass container in the refrigerator and eat within 3 days. Frozen leftovers will keep for up to 3 months.

~~~~~~~~~

power food tip *Add 1 extra tablespoon (15 mL) grated ginger for a little extra kick to your soup.*

4 cups (1 L) butternut squash, peeled and chopped

1 apple, cored and diced

¼ cup (60 mL) cashews, ground

½ tsp (2 mL) grated ginger

1 tsp (5 mL) cinnamon

½ tsp (2 mL) nutmeg

½ tsp (2 mL) Himalayan crystal salt

1 cup (250 mL) apple juice

1 cup (250 mL) water

GINGER CURRY SOUP

MAKES 10 CUPS (2.5 L)

PLACE ALL THE INGREDIENTS, except the garnish, into a blender and blend until smooth. Once blended, eat as a cold soup or, alternatively, heat the soup in a large saucepan over medium heat until it reaches your desired temperature. Stir continuously to avoid burning the bottom and to evenly warm throughout. Garnish each serving with some crushed cashews and freshly grated ginger.

~~~~~~~~~

power food tip If you do not have a high-speed blender, you can place all the ingredients into a saucepan and use a hand blender to purée your soup. The warmer the soup becomes, the easier you will find it to blend the soup with a hand blender.

3 apples, diced

4 carrots, diced

1 onion, diced

2 cloves garlic, minced

½ cup (125 mL) parsley, chopped

1 cup (250 mL) cashews

1 cup (250 mL) hemp seeds

1 tbsp (15 mL) lemon juice

1 tbsp (15 mL) grated ginger

2 tbsp (30 mL) curry powder

1 tsp (5 mL) Himalayan crystal salt

½ tsp (2 mL) ground black pepper

6 cups (1.5 L) water

Crushed cashews and extra grated
   ginger for garnish

RED PEPPER AND HEMP GINGER SOUP

MAKES 4 CUPS (1 L)

PLACE ALL THE INGREDIENTS, except the garnish, into a blender and blend until smooth. Add more water as needed until the soup reaches your desired consistency. This is a cold soup. If you prefer it warm, heat it in a saucepan over low heat while stirring continuously. Garnish with 1 tbsp (15 mL) hemp seeds and 1 tbsp (15 mL) chopped oregano.

≈≈≈

power food tip *Add ¼ cup (60 mL) ground almonds to each serving to give this soup a very nice crunch.*

2 large red peppers, seeded and
  chopped
½ cup (125 mL) hemp seeds
2 tbsp (30 mL) lemon juice
½ tsp (2 mL) grated ginger
½ tsp (2 mL) curry powder
½ tsp (2 mL) cumin
½ tsp (2 mL) caraway seeds, ground
½ tsp (2 mL) Himalayan crystal salt
1 tsp (5 mL) ground black pepper
½ cup (125 mL) water
Extra hemp seeds and fresh oregano
  for garnish

THE POWER OF GARLIC

WHY YOU SHOULD CARE In recent years you may have read in the news that we are on the verge of breeding a new line of superbugs due to our overdependence on antibiotics. There is a lot of fear around this information, but there is also some truth to it. Antibiotics play an important role in the health of our community, but there is no question they are also overprescribed. Since I began researching nutrition over 10 years ago, I have not used antibiotics once. I am not saying I may never need them again, but I have learned that food has much more power then I ever gave it credit for. Garlic's natural antibiotic properties have made it one of our family's go-to foods. When any of us feels a viral infection coming on, we introduce garlic into our diet multiple times a day. The next time you find yourself running to the washroom with a bladder infection, give your immune system a powerful boost with some fresh garlic.

HOW TO USE Eating fresh garlic is the ideal way to benefit from its healthful properties. You can also find it as a powder, in flakes, as an extract, in pill form, as oil and as a paste. Avoid buying fresh garlic that appears mouldy, dried out or soft. I find that the best-quality garlic is super sticky when peeled.

Breakfast: Garlic makes a great addition to an early-morning vegetable juice. I also enjoy lots of garlic when I make home-baked breakfast potatoes.

Lunch/Snack: Garlic is a main ingredient in many of my dip, sauce and spread recipes. It also adds flavour to salad dressings and soups.

Dinner: Pasta, stews, pizza, garlic bread, veggie burgers, stir-fries—all need garlic. You name the dish, and garlic should be part of it. Garlic makes a flavourful and healthy addition to any of your kitchen creations.

HOW TO STORE Store fresh garlic bulbs in a paper bag in the cupboard, away from any heat source. This helps maintain freshness and prevents the garlic from sprouting too soon. Garlic will keep up to 30 days, but that time depends on how fresh it was when purchased. Once you peel the outer skin and expose garlic to the air, you have 2 to 3 days before it begins to dry out.

Garlic, that instantly recognizable bulb in the onion family, is most known for its ability to ward off vampires—and perhaps your co-workers or loved ones as well—but it is the health benefits of garlic that put it on my list of Power Foods. In addition to being a good source of vitamin C and selenium, garlic can help with iron metabolism. It has also been shown to be a strong natural broad-spectrum antibiotic.

HEALTHY GARLIC SAUCE

MAKES 4 CUPS (1 L)

PLACE ALL THE INGREDIENTS into a food processor and blend together until smooth. Add more water as needed until the sauce reaches your desired consistency. Store any leftovers in an airtight glass container in the refrigerator and consume within 4 days.

≈≈≈≈

power food tip *I use this sauce as a vegetable dip or as a spread, smeared over my veggie crackers, on toast or inside some lettuce as a wrap. Give it try.*

2 cups (500 mL) artichoke hearts

1 tomato, diced

1 onion, diced

1 clove garlic, minced

¼ cup (60 mL) radish, chopped

½ cup (125 mL) dill, chopped

½ cup (125 mL) mint, chopped

Juice of 1 lemon

½ cup (125 mL) hemp seeds

1 tsp (5 mL) grated ginger

1 tbsp (15 mL) prepared mustard

1 tsp (5 mL) turmeric

1 tsp (5 mL) Himalayan crystal salt

1 tsp (5 mL) ground black pepper

¼ cup (60 mL) water

VEGGIETASTIC QUESADILLA

MAKES 1 SERVING

PLACE THE OLIVE OIL into a large frying pan with a lid over low heat. Next, place the brown rice wrap into the oiled pan. Place all the filling ingredients evenly over one half of the wrap. Then fold the other side of the wrap onto the ingredients and press firmly. Let the wrap cook slowly for 2 to 3 minutes over low heat. Flip the wrap over and cook for another 2 to 3 minutes. Once done, cut the quesadilla into 2 wedges and serve.

≈≈≈≈

power food tip *Eat this tasty wrap with a homemade salsa or guacamole. Try Tropical Salsa (page 140) or Go-Time Guacamole (page 146).*

1 tbsp (15 mL) extra virgin olive oil

1 brown rice wrap

FILLING

¼ cup (60 mL) black beans, mashed

¼ cup (60 mL) spinach

¼ red pepper, seeded and diced

¼ onion, diced

1 clove garlic, minced

1 tbsp (15 mL) hemp seeds

PICK-ME-UP SOUP

MAKES 6 CUPS (1.5 L)

PLACE ALL THE INGREDIENTS into a food processor or blender and blend until smooth. Before serving, drizzle with additional olive oil for added taste and essential fatty acids. This is a cold soup. If you prefer it warm, heat it in a saucepan over low heat while stirring continuously. Store any leftovers in an airtight glass container in the refrigerator and eat within 3 days. Frozen leftovers will keep for up to 3 months.

≋≋≋

power food tip *Add any combination of ground nuts or seeds to this soup to change the flavour, boost the nutritional value as well as alter the texture, as you wish.*

2 large tomatoes, diced

1 cucumber, diced

1 avocado, peeled, pitted and chopped

3 handfuls fresh spinach

1 clove garlic, minced

½ cup (125 mL) cilantro, chopped

¼ cup (60 mL) dill, chopped

2 tbsp (30 mL) extra virgin olive oil

2 pinches cayenne pepper

Pinch Himalayan crystal salt

1½ cups (375 mL) water

RAWKIN CRACKER TOPPING

MAKES 6 CUPS (1.5 L)

PLACE ALL THE INGREDIENTS into a large mixing bowl and gently mix together. Add 1 tbsp (15 mL) as a garnish to a bowl of Silky-Smooth Cauliflower Soup (page 185) or spread this topping on Super Veggie Quinoa Crackers (page 171).

≋≋≋

power food tip *Add ¼ cup (60 mL) ground almonds to give this topping a little extra crunch.*

½ red pepper, seeded and diced

½ yellow pepper, seeded and diced

1 red onion, diced

1 clove garlic, minced

¼ cup (60 mL) parsley, chopped

¼ cup (60 mL) hemp seeds

2 tbsp (30 mL) extra virgin olive oil

Juice of 1 lemon

½ tsp (2 mL) Himalayan crystal salt

Pinch ground black pepper

PARSLEY MANGO SUNSET SALAD

MAKES 6 SERVINGS

SOAK THE GOJI BERRIES in 1 cup (250 mL) water for 20 minutes. After the berries have soaked, drain them, discarding the water. Place the soaked berries with the remaining ingredients into a large mixing bowl and gently combine. Refrigerate the salad for 30 minutes and then serve. Store any leftovers in an airtight glass container in the refrigerator for up to 3 days. This salad pairs really well with Ultimate Veggie Burgers (page 73).

≈≈≈≈≈

power food tip *Serve this salad inside a large piece of Swiss chard or kale to increase the nutritional value and to play with the presentation. This idea also makes a great wrap alternative for lunch or dinner.*

½ cup (125 mL) dried goji berries

2 avocados, peeled, pitted and diced

1 mango, peeled and chopped

Juice of 1 grapefruit

Juice of 2 lemons

4 tomatoes, diced

3 celery stalks, chopped

1 cup (250 mL) parsley, chopped

½ onion, diced

1 clove garlic, minced

½ cup (125 mL) olives, chopped

1 cup (250 mL) walnuts

1 cup (250 mL) hemp seeds

1 tbsp (15 mL) grated ginger

1 tsp (5 mL) turmeric

1 tsp (5 mL) ground black pepper

NUDE PAD THAI

MAKES 6 SERVINGS

NOODLES Using the large spiral blade on a Spirooli vegetable slicer, slice the zucchini and set aside in a bowl. If you do not have a Spirooli slicer, grate the zucchini using a cheese grater.

SAUCE Place all the sauce ingredients into a food processor and blend until well combined. Pour the sauce over the prepared zucchini.

GARNISH Add the garnish ingredients overtop.

~~~~~~~~~

power food tip *Add an extra ½ cup (125 mL) cashews to the blended sauce mix to turn the sauce into a creamy, rich vegetable dip.*

NOODLES
2 medium zucchini

SAUCE
2 pitted dates, chopped
½ cup (125 mL) almond butter
2 tbsp (30 mL) lemon juice
1 tbsp (15 mL) soy sauce
2 cloves garlic, minced
1 tsp (5 mL) grated ginger
1 tsp (5 mL) jalapeño, minced
½ cup (125 mL) cashews
½ tsp (2 mL) cayenne pepper
½ cup (125 mL) coconut milk

GARNISH
½ cup (125 mL) tomatoes, diced
½ cup (125 mL) red peppers, seeded
  and diced
1 cup (250 mL) almonds, roasted
  and crushed
½ cup (125 mL) hemp seeds

THE POWER OF BEETS

WHY YOU SHOULD CARE For years I spent a lot of time, energy and money trying to lose weight. Beyond dieting, I looked to cleansing for some solutions to my weight problems. When cleansing, you really need to know what you are doing to keep it safe, plus cleanses are not always cheap. From my own, unprepared experiences, I can say that the cleanses I did were not very successful. This was mainly because every time I completed a cleanse, I went back to eating the same types of processed foods. Unfortunately, I didn't know any different, and even though a particular cleanse might have helped me lose a few pounds, I would always gain the weight back when I returned to my former diet. Those days are long gone, and I now see the benefits of cleansing *only if* you know what you are doing. Being well informed about how your cleanse might impact your health as well as how to transition off your cleanse is crucial to ensuring you maintain results long term. Recently I have turned to beets as a big part of my cleansing routine. Due to the betalin pigments that give them their colour, beets act as a detoxifier and neutralize toxins, making them easy to eliminate through your urine. If you are worried about the buildup of toxins in your body and want a powerful food to help eliminate them, beets should be a part of your daily diet.

HOW TO USE Beets are available in their whole state, as a powder or as beet sugar. You can also consume the leaves, which are full of nutritional value but are a little bitter in taste. Look for beets that are hard and solid, not dry and soft. Beets are a delicate food and heat sensitive. I try to dice beets along with their leaves into many of my recipes to enjoy their full benefit.

Breakfast: Add some diced beets to your smoothie or grate some onto toast with almond butter.

Lunch/Snack: Sliced or grated beats make a colourful addition to any soup, salad, sandwich or wrap.

Dinner: Get creative with tonight's dinner by using the leaves of beets as a wrap. Fill your wrap with one of my Power of Food dips and some extra grated beets for an easy and healthy meal. Beets also work well in stews, as a pizza topping, in veggie burgers or in vegetable shepherd's pie.

HOW TO STORE The life of your beet will depend on its state when you received it. If you can, purchase beets that are firm, with no soft or dry spots or bruises. I once tried freezing beets to preserve them longer, but they thawed out very soft. Fresh beets should be stored in an airtight bag in the vegetable crisper of your refrigerator. They will keep for up to 2 weeks if stored properly.

Beets make my list of top Power Foods for several reasons. I like beets not only because they are a great source of fibre, vitamin C, iron and potassium, but also because of their colour. Ranging from gold through ruby-red to deepest magenta, beets bedazzle the eye come late summer at your local farmers' market. The pigment that gives beets their rich colour is a phytonutrient that provides antioxidants, decreases inflammation and aids in cleansing unwanted waste from your body. Now that's a power food.

YOU'VE GONE CRACKERS

MAKES 16 TO 24 CRACKERS

PLACE ALL THE INGREDIENTS into a food processor and blend together. Once blended, spread the mixture evenly on a dehydrator tray. Use 2 or 3 trays to be able to evenly spread the mixture to your desired thickness. The thicker the cracker, the longer it takes to dehydrate or bake. Dehydrate at 105°F (41°C) for 6 hours, then flip the cracker over and dehydrate for another 6 hours. If using an oven, bake at the lowest temperature for 30 minutes on one side and 30 minutes on the other. If still moist after 1 hour of baking, flip over the crackers and bake until they reach your desired crispness. Once done, break your crackers into bite-size pieces to enjoy as desired. Stored in an airtight glass container in the cupboard, these crackers will keep for 7 to 10 days. Try adding a little Rawkin Cracker Topping (page 177) or crumble some crackers overtop of my Red Pepper and Hemp Ginger Soup (page 174).

≈≈≈≈≈

power food tip *I like to make a large batch of these crackers and freeze them in an airtight glass container to have for quick, on-the-go healthy snacks. They will keep in the freezer for up to 6 months.*

4 carrots, chopped

4 celery stalks, chopped

1 beet, shredded

1 onion, diced

¼ cucumber, diced

¼ cup (60 mL) parsley, diced

¼ cup (60 mL) basil, diced

1 cup (250 mL) hemp seeds

¼ cup (60 mL) caraway seeds, ground

1 tsp (5 mL) Himalayan crystal salt

RAWTASTIC PIZZA

MAKES TWO 8-INCH (20 CM) ROUND PIZZAS

CRUST Place all the crust ingredients into a food processor and blend together. Once blended, spread the mixture evenly into an 8-inch (20 cm) round shape on a dehydrator tray. Dehydrate at 115°F (46°C) for 6 hours, then flip the crust over and dehydrate for another 6 hours. If using an oven, spread the mixture onto a baking sheet lined with parchment paper or waxed paper and bake at the lowest temperature for 30 minutes. If the crust is still moist after this time, bake for an additional 30 minutes, or until the crust reaches your desired crispness.

SAUCE Place all the sauce ingredients into a food processor and blend together. Once blended, spread the sauce over the already dehydrated or baked pizza crust.

TOPPINGS I like adding chopped olives, garlic, tomatoes, beets, broccoli, spinach and red peppers to my pizza. Think of the endless combination of vegetables, nuts and seeds you can add. Be sure to spread your toppings evenly over your pizza. This is a healthy cold pizza, but it can be heated in your oven if desired.

～～～～～

power food tip *Before serving, drizzle over each slice of pizza 1 tbsp (15 mL) hemp oil to enrich the flavour and provide a healthy dose of omega-3 and omega-6 oils.*

CRUST

2 cups (500 mL) zucchini, diced

½ beet, shredded

3 cups (750 mL) flaxseeds, ground

½ cup (125 mL) sunflower seeds

1 cup (250 mL) water

SAUCE

4 tomatoes, chopped

1 beet, grated

1 can (14 oz/398 mL) chickpeas

3 cloves garlic, minced

1 tbsp (15 mL) grated ginger

1 tbsp (15 mL) tahini

¼ cup (60 mL) almonds

½ tsp (2 mL) cayenne pepper

½ tsp (2 mL) curry powder

1 tbsp (15 mL) Himalayan crystal salt

1 tsp (5 mL) ground black pepper

TOPPINGS

2 cups (500 mL) diced vegetables of your choice

CUCUMBER AND BASIL SALAD

MAKES 4 SERVINGS

PLACE ALL THE INGREDIENTS except the hemp seeds into a mixing bowl and gently combine. Add ¼ cup (60 mL), hemp seeds to this salad, if using, and enjoy as the perfect healthy lunch or dinner.

〰️

power food tip *Garnish with ¼ cup (60 mL) dried cranberries to sweeten your salad while adding a little colour to your plate.*

1 cucumber, diced

2 tomatoes, diced

¼ cup (60 mL) basil, chopped

¼ cup (60 mL) flax oil

2 tbsp (30 mL) lemon juice

½ tsp (2 mL) Himalayan crystal salt

½ tsp (2 mL) ground black pepper

¼ cup (60 mL) hemp seeds (optional)

SILKY-SMOOTH CAULIFLOWER SOUP

MAKES 6 CUPS (1.5 L)

SOAK THE CASHEWS in 1 cup (250 mL) water for 30 minutes. Once they have soaked, drain the cashews, discarding the water. Place the soaked cashews and the remaining ingredients, except the garnish, into a blender or food processor and blend until silky smooth. Add more hemp milk if you want your soup a little more runny. This is a cold soup. If you prefer it warm, heat it in a saucepan over low heat while stirring continuously. Garnish each serving with 1 tbsp (15 mL) crushed cashews. Store any leftovers in an airtight glass container in the refrigerator and eat within 3 days. Frozen leftovers will keep for up to 3 months.

〰️

power food tip *Add 2 soaked and chopped pitted dates to the blender to add a little sweetness to this soup. You could also try adding ¼ tsp (1 mL) cayenne pepper to supply a hit of heat.*

½ cup (125 mL) cashews

½ cauliflower, chopped

½ small onion, diced

2 tbsp (30 mL) flax oil

2 tbsp (30 mL) hemp oil

1 tbsp (15 mL) lemon juice

1 tbsp (15 mL) caraway seeds, ground

½ tsp (2 mL) nutmeg

½ tsp (2 mL) Himalayan crystal salt

½ tsp (2 mL) ground black pepper

1 cup (250 mL) hemp milk (page 81)

Extra crushed cashews for garnish

LUSCIOUS ZUCCHINI AND SPINACH SOUP

MAKES 4 CUPS (1 L)

PLACE ALL THE INGREDIENTS, except the garnish, into a blender and blend until smooth. This is a cold soup. If you prefer it warm, heat it in a saucepan over low heat while stirring continuously. Garnish each serving with 1 tbsp (15 mL) crushed almonds to add a little crunch. Store any leftovers in an airtight glass container in the refrigerator and eat within 3 days. Frozen leftovers will keep for up to 3 months.

power food tip *Add a peeled, chopped avocado to increase the thickness and creaminess of this soup if desired.*

2 cups (500 mL) zucchini, chopped

1½ cups (375 mL) fresh spinach

¼ cup (60 mL) dill, chopped

1 tbsp (15 mL) flax oil

1 tbsp (15 mL) lemon juice

1 tbsp (15 mL) tahini

½ tsp (2 mL) Himalayan crystal salt

1 cup (250 mL) water

Crushed almonds for garnish

YUMMY YAM FRIES

MAKES 4 SERVINGS

PREHEAT THE OVEN to 350°F (180°C). Slice the yams into thin pieces like french fries. In a large mixing bowl, using a fork, mix together the oil, salt and pepper. Next add the yams and mix using a spatula, until all the pieces are well coated. Add more oil if needed. Place the yams on a baking tray and bake for 30 minutes, or until a little golden brown. This family-friendly recipe goes great beside my Ultimate Veggie Burgers (page 73).

2 large yams, peeled

¼ cup (60 mL) extra virgin olive oil

1 tsp (5 mL) Himalayan crystal salt

1 tbsp (15 mL) ground black pepper

~~~~~~

power food tip   *Add 2 tbsp (30 mL) cayenne pepper into the oil mix to spice up your yam fries.*

SWEET POTATO AND TURNIP MASH

MAKES 6 CUPS (1.5 L)

IN A LARGE VEGETABLE STEAMER, steam the potatoes and turnips until tender, about 20 minutes. After the vegetables are soft, place them with the remaining ingredients into a food processor and blend until smooth. Add more hemp milk as needed until the mash reaches your desired consistency.

5 sweet potatoes, peeled and chopped

3 large turnips, peeled and chopped

2 tbsp (30 mL) prepared mustard

2 tbsp (30 mL) flax oil

1 tbsp (15 mL) honey

½ tsp (2 mL) nutmeg

½ tsp (2 mL) Himalayan crystal salt

½ tsp (2 mL) ground black pepper

¼ hemp milk (page 81)

~~~~~~

power food tip   *For a touch of elegance, serve this mash in individual wine glasses at your next party, topped with a spoonful of Heart-Healthy Gravy (page 128). You will be a crowd favourite.*

BEYOND

THE POWER

OF FOOD

THE GREATEST NEWS ABOUT spending time in your kitchen preparing healthy, tasty recipes is that the more you do it, the easier it becomes—especially if you are doing it from a place of love, care and respect. I want this ease of creating in your kitchen to happen for you, and the Power of Food recipes will help make it happen. Being in my kitchen has become a very big act of love for myself. This starts right from the moment I think about creating a recipe. Going out to buy the ingredients, I mindfully give thanks to each food. Preparing the ingredients and preparing each recipe—even cleaning up—I consider all of this an act of love. When I am eating my creations, I am extra mindful of how each bite nourishes my body and mind. I take time to chew, I visualize nutrients being absorbed into my bloodstream, and I often engage my five senses while enjoying the pleasures of eating living food.

All of this may sound slightly "out there," I realize. In the past my own internal saboteur would have dismissed the idea of loving myself in such a way. However, since this approach allows me to live abundantly happy and healthy, I truly believe it will work for you as well. The recipes in *The Power of Food* are perfect for helping you to get creative with your food and strengthen the power of self-love in every action you take.

ACTION STEP 12.
LOVE YOUR FOOD

Getting to love my food was something that evolved for me over the years. The more I spent time in my kitchen nourishing myself with living foods, the more I became mindful of how each moment in the process of selecting and preparing that food was a very powerful act of love for myself. As my mindfulness grew around the process I outline below, I began to live with less stress and more abundant energy and happiness.

1. Pick a Power of Food recipe to make.
2. On a piece of paper or in your Power of Food Notebook, list of all the actions needed to complete the recipe. These might include making a grocery list, going out to buy the foods, washing the food, cutting and dicing the food, preparing the recipe, eating the food and cleaning up afterwards.
3. Be extra mindful of each moment spent during the recipe process as a very big act of love you are giving yourself. When walking, biking, driving or taking the bus to your grocery store, breathe in the positive vibrations. When you touch the food and put it into your basket or cart, give thanks for how it will nourish

you. As you prepare the recipe, spend the entire time being mindful of how the whole process represents an act of love, care and respect for yourself.

4. While eating your creation, engage your five senses. Spend 5 to 10 seconds focusing on each one. Look at the food closely, feel the texture and taste as you put it in your mouth, put it to your nose and inhale deeply. As you chew the food, what do you hear?

5. When cleaning up your meal, be extra mindful of how this too represents an act of love, and breathe deeply while you clear the table and wash the dishes.

6. After you have finished cleaning up your creation, go into your "My First Ten" practice space. Visualize the recipe sequence (steps 2 to 5) and how each step made you feel.

7. After visualizing the process, on a piece of paper or in your Power of Food Notebook, below where you wrote the list of actions needed to complete the recipe, spend two minutes writing about how this action step made you feel. Give it everything you've got.

8. Repeat steps 1 to 7 two more times this week.

WHAT YOU CAN EXPECT: This exercise will help to reawaken your relationship to food. It will help you start to feel more energized and nourished through everything you do in your life. On a cellular level, practising this action step will power up your immune system and lower your cortisol (stress hormone) levels, leading to fewer food cravings and an easier ability to lose weight.

TOP FIVE STEPS TO MAKING YOUR RESULTS COUNT

Will this be another year where you wonder how January came along and still you have not begun to take action toward losing those few pounds? How did you feel the last time you started a diet or exercise routine with great intentions, but only found yourself failing to see permanent results yet again? *Why can't I get healthy? When is this tire around my gut going to disappear? I'm so tired of feeling tired all the time.* If any of these thoughts sound familiar to you, it's time to make your results count!

I know from personal experience that it is not easy to achieve results unless you are willing to make an effort to ensure success. There is no quick fix, and relying on one-dimensional solutions will only keep you locked in an unhealthy state. *The Power of Food* is your main resource for your continued drive toward better health. Following the 12 action steps explained in this book will ensure you achieve your desired results.

Now that you have a clear understanding of the important role your intentions play in your success, how being in nature nurtures you ability to bring your intentions to life and how the power of food fuels you from the inside out, I want to leave you with my five key steps that will help you stay the course and begin experiencing the results you desire within a matter of days. These five key steps recap many of the 12 action steps and help summarize how to begin taking action for abundant health and happiness the minute you put down this book. Use these five key steps as a guide to moving forward *right now*.

1. SET YOUR 5-YEAR INTENTIONS

Firstly you need to set your 5-year intentions (see Action Step 3, page 11). What is it you truly want? How would you like to feel every day? Setting your intentions is like building the foundation for you to experience abundant health and happiness. If I told you that doing this simple exercise is your key to unlocking everything you want

in life, would you give it all your attention, energy and focus for the next few minutes? By setting your intentions, you will strengthen your opportunity to achieve the results you desire. If you have not done so already, now is the time for you to detail inside your Power of Food Notebook what it is you truly want in your life. See Action Step 3 (page 11) for full details.

2. PRACTISE "MY FIRST TEN"

Once you have set your 5-year intentions, begin engaging your energy through practising "My First Ten," introduced in Action Step 6 (page 19). Get started right away for speedier results. Don't forget to pay attention to everything that happens throughout your day. Every phone call, every email, every conversation plays a role in your intentions becoming reality. Everything happens for a reason!

Here are several pointers to ensure you maximize your potential while practising "My First Ten." First, create a safe, quiet and comfortable personal space where you will not be disturbed during your practice. Find a place where you can begin to build your daily "My First Ten" practice. Your ideal space is somewhere where you can post materials on the walls and be free of distractions.

As you spend more time in your space, it will evolve. Be mindful of all the tools, materials and equipment you will want on hand to ensure you continue on with your practice each morning. Items might include your Power of Food Notebook, a pencil or pen, a cushion to sit on, your vision board materials, and so on. Gather all the materials needed to engage in your practice, so you can practise "My First Ten" every morning without anything holding you back.

If there are a few things you *need* to do in order to be fully present during your "My First Ten" practice, take care of them before you practise. Take a shower, wash your face or brush your teeth—these are acceptable. Getting a cup of coffee is not. It is important that you begin your daily practice as soon as possible each morning. Being aware of this, you will be the judge of your starting point.

Finally, if you miss a day of practising "My First Ten," don't worry about it. You are allowed to miss as many days as you want. There is no pressure to do anything. Just know that the more you practise, the more powerful and more effortless these 10 minutes become.

3. ENGAGE IN AN OUTDOOR ACTIVITY

Now that you have set your intentions as well as begun practising "My First Ten" daily, find an outdoor activity to increase your time spent being with nature. It does not matter what you choose to do as long as it gets you outside for a few minutes several times a week. Trail running, road jogging, golf, tennis, biking or taking evening walks are all great activates to get you outside. It is important to be mindful, while you are engaged in your outdoor activity, to the power of being with nature. As much as possible, practise being with nature during your outdoor activities. This can be done before or after you begin your activity. See Action Step 4 (page 14).

4. LOVE THE POWER OF FOOD

Right now is your time to shine. Every day, strive to meet the Magic Number of 51%. Keep adding in your chosen Power Foods daily and get creative with your Power of Food recipes often to begin living the 80/20 rule. Use your Power of Food *Daily Food Journal* to track your progress, and practise loving your food with Action Step 12 (page 189) several times each week.

5. GET SUPPORT

The systems, tools and action steps in this book are a lot of fun to activate. And one way to maximize their potential is to find a partner to enjoy them with. Having someone with whom you can share your successes and talk in times of need is crucial to ensure you stay committed and turn your new love for yourself into a lifestyle. Support could come from a loving family member, a good friend, a personal trainer or a coach. No matter where your support comes from, it is important to share your intentions with someone who will provide encouragement along the way.

Follow these five key steps daily. If you do, you will be sure to attain abundant health and happiness with ease. I thank you for picking up *The Power of Food*. I encourage you to share it with a loved one. I would love to hear from you about your experience of reading this book, trying the recipes and learning to love the power of living foods. I look forward to meeting you in person at a Power of Food live event and having you as part of the Power of Food community.

Your friend in health,

Adam Hart

To comment, please visit the following:

WEBSITE   PowerofFood.com/blog

FACEBOOK   Power of Food or Adam Hart

TWITTER   Power of Food

EMAIL   adam@poweroffood.com

INDEX

Adam Hart's
POWER OF FOOD

Daily Food Journal

Date:

Today I ate	Living Food ✓	Processed Food ✗
	Total ✓	**Total ✗**
My daily total	_____	

If you have more ✓ than ✗ you are above 51%. What was your % for the day?